Pushing to the Front

Volume 3

Orison Swett Marden

Pushing to the Front
or, Success under Difficulties

Volume THREE: Chapters 35 thru 50

Orison Swett Marden

Author of *Architects of Fate, or, Steps to Success and Power*, and *How to Succeed, or, Stepping-Stones to Fame and Fortune*.

© 2023 Editorial RENUEVO, LLC

ISBN: 978-1-64142-392-2

Published by
Editorial RENUEVO, LLC.
www.EditorialRenuevo.com
info@EditorialRenuevo.com

CONTENTS

Foreword

This revised and greatly enlarged edition of *Pushing to the Front* is the outgrowth of an almost worldwide demand for an extension of the idea which made the original small volume such an ambition-arousing, energizing, inspiring force.

It has sent thousands of youths, with renewed determination, back to school or college, back to all sorts of vocations which they had abandoned in moments of discouragement. It has kept scores of business men from failure after they had given up all hope.

It has helped multitudes of poor boys and girls to pay their way through college who had never thought a liberal education possible.

The author has received thousands of letters from people in nearly all parts of the world telling how the book has aroused their ambition, changed their ideals and aims, and has spurred them to the successful undertaking of what they before had thought impossible.

The book has been translated into many foreign languages. In Japan and several other countries, it is used extensively in the public schools.

Distinguished educators in many parts of the world have recommended its use in schools as a civilization builder.

Crowned heads, presidents of republics, distinguished members of the British and other parliaments, members of the United States Supreme Court, noted authors, scholars, and eminent people in many parts of the world, have eulogized this book and have thanked the author for giving it to the world.

This volume is full of the most fascinating romances of achievement under difficulties, of obscure beginnings and triumphant endings, of stirring stories of struggles and triumphs. It gives inspiring stories of men and women who have brought great things to pass. It gives numerous examples of the triumph of mediocrity, showing how those of ordinary ability have succeeded by the use of ordinary means. It shows how invalids and cripples even have triumphed by perseverance and will over seemingly insuperable difficulties.

The book tells how men and women have seized common occasions and made them great; it tells of those of average ability who have succeeded by the use of ordinary means, by dint of indomitable will and inflexible purpose. It tells how poverty and hardship have rocked the cradle of the giants of the race. The book points out that most people do not utilize a large part of their effort because their mental attitude does not correspond with their endeavor, so that although working for one thing, they are really expecting something else; and it is what we expect that we tend to get.

No man can become prosperous while he really expects or half expects to remain poor, for holding the poverty thought, keeping in touch with poverty-producing conditions, discourages prosperity.

Before a man can lift himself, he must lift his thoughts. When we shall have learned to master our thought habits, to keep our minds open to the great divine inflow of life force, we shall have learned the truths of human endowment, human possibility.

The book points out the fact that what is called success may be failure; that when men love money so much that they sacrifice their friendships, their families, their home life, sacrifice position, honor, health, everything for the dollar, their life is a failure, although they may have accumulated money. It shows how men have become rich at the price of their ideals, their character, at the cost of everything noblest, best, and truest in life. It preaches the larger doctrine of equality; the equality of will and purpose which paves a clear path even to the Presidential chair for a Lincoln or a Garfield, for anyone who will pay the price of study and struggle.

Men who feel themselves badly handicapped, crippled by their lack of early education, will find in these pages great encouragement to broaden their horizon, and will get a practical, helpful, sensible education in their odd moments and half-holidays.

Dr. Marden, in *Pushing to the Front*, shows that the average of the leaders are not above the average of ability. They are ordinary people, but of extraordinary persistence and perseverance. It is a storehouse of noble incentive, a treasury of precious sayings. There is inspiration and encouragement and helpfulness on every page. It teaches the doctrine that no limits can be placed on one's career if he has once learned the alphabet and has push; that there are no barriers that can say to aspiring talent, "Thus far, and no farther."

Encouragement is its keynote; it aims to arouse to honorable exertion those who are drifting without aim, to awaken dormant ambitions in those who have grown discouraged in the struggle for success.

The Publisher

Chapter
35

GETTING AROUSED

"How's the boy gittin' on, Davis?" asked Farmer John Field, as he watched his son, Marshall, waiting upon a customer. "Well, John, you and I are old friends," replied Deacon Davis, as he took an apple from a barrel and handed it to Marshall's father as a peace offering; "we are old friends, and I don't want to hurt your feelings; but I'm a blunt man, and air goin' to tell you the truth. Marshall is a good, steady boy, all right, but he wouldn't make a merchant if he stayed in my store a thousand years. If he weren't cut out for a merchant. Take him back to the farm, John, and teach him how to milk cows!"

If Marshall Field had remained as clerk in Deacon Davis's store in Pittsfield, Massachusetts, where he got his first position, he could never have become one of the world's merchant princes. But when he went to Chicago and saw the marvelous examples around him of poor boys who had won success, it aroused his ambition and fired him with the determination to be a great merchant himself. "If others can do such wonderful things," he asked himself, "why cannot I?"

Of course, there was the making of a great merchant in Mr. Field from the start; but circumstances, an ambition-arousing environment, had a great deal to do with stimulating his latent energy and bringing out his reserve force. It is doubtful if he would have climbed so rapidly in any other place than Chicago. In 1856, when young Field went there, this marvelous city was just starting on its unparalleled career. It had then only about 85,000 inhabitants. A few years before it had been a mere Indian trading village. But the city grew by leaps and bounds, and always beat the predictions of its most sanguine inhabitants. Success was in the air. Everybody felt that there were great possibilities there.

Marshall Field

Many people seem to think that ambition is a quality born within us; that it is not susceptible to improvement; that it is something thrust upon us which will take care of itself. But it is a passion that responds very quickly to cultivation, and it requires constant care and education, just as the faculty for music or art does, or it will atrophy.

If we do not try to realize our ambition, it will not keep sharp and defined. Our faculties become dull and soon lose their power if they are not exercised. How can we expect our ambition to remain fresh and vigorous through years of inactivity, indolence, or indifference? If we constantly allow opportunities to slip by us without making any attempt to grasp them, our inclination will grow duller and weaker.

"What I most need," as Emerson says, "is somebody to make me do what I can." To do what I can, that is my problem; not what a Napoleon or a Lincoln could do, but what I can do. It makes all the difference in the world to me whether I bring out the best thing in me or the worst—whether I utilize 10, 15, 25, or 90 percent of my ability.

Everywhere we see people who have reached middle life or later without being aroused. They have developed only a small percentage of their success possibilities. They are still in a dormant state. The best thing in them lies so deep that it has never been awakened. When we meet these people, we feel conscious that they have a great deal of latent power that has never been exercised. Great possibilities of usefulness and of achievement are, all unconsciously, going to waste within them.

Some time ago there appeared in the newspapers an account of a girl who had reached the age of 15 years, and yet had only attained the mental development of a small child. Only a few things interested her. She was dreamy, inactive, and indifferent to everything around her most of the time until, one day, while listening to a hand organ on the street, she suddenly awakened to full consciousness. She came to herself; her faculties were aroused, and in a few days, she leaped forward years in her development. Almost in a day she passed from childhood to budding womanhood. Most of us have an enormous amount of power, of latent force, slumbering within us, as it slumbered in this girl, which could do marvels if we would only awaken it.

The judge of the municipal court in a flourishing western city, one of the most highly esteemed jurists in his state, was in middle life, before his latent power was aroused, an illiterate blacksmith. He is now 60, the owner of the finest library in his city, with the reputation of being its best-read man, and one whose highest endeavor is to help his fellow man. What caused the revolution in his life? The hearing of a single lecture on the value of education. This was what stirred the slumbering power within him, awakened his ambition, and set his feet in the path of self-development.

I have known several men who never realized their possibilities until they reached middle life. Then they were suddenly aroused, as if from a long sleep, by reading some inspiring, stimulating book, by listening to a sermon or a lecture, or by meeting some friend, someone with high ideals, who understood, believed in, and encouraged them.

It will make all the difference in the world to you whether you are with people who are watching for ability in you, people who believe in, encourage, and praise you, or whether you are with those who are forever breaking your idols, blasting your hopes, and throwing cold water on your aspirations.

The chief probation officer of the children's court in New York, in his report for 1905, says: "Removing a boy or girl from improper environment is the first step in his or her reclamation." The New York Society for the Prevention of Cruelty to Children, after 30 years of investigation of cases involving the social and moral welfare of over half a million of children, has also come to the conclusion that environment is stronger than heredity.

Even the strongest of us are not beyond the reach of our environment. No matter how independent, strong-willed, and determined our nature, we are constantly being modified by our surroundings. Take the best-born child, with the greatest inherited advantages, and let it be reared by savages, and how many of its inherited tendencies will remain? If brought up from infancy in a barbarous, brutal atmosphere, it will, of course, become brutal. The story is told of a wellborn child who, being lost or abandoned as an infant, was suckled by a wolf with her own young ones, and who actually took on all the characteristics of the wolf—walked on all fours, howled like a wolf, and ate like one.

It does not take much to determine the lives of most of us. We naturally follow the examples about us, and, as a rule, we rise or fall according to the strongest current in which we live. The poet's "I am a part of all that I have met" is not a mere poetic flight of fancy; it is an absolute truth. Everything—every sermon or lecture or conversation you have heard, every person who has touched your life—has left an impress upon your character, and you are never quite the same person after the association or experience. You are a little different, modified somewhat from what you were before—just as Beecher was never the same man after reading Ruskin.

Some years ago, a party of Russian workmen were sent to this country by a Russian firm of shipbuilders, in order that they might acquire American methods and catch the American spirit. Within six months the Russians had become almost the equals of the American artisans among whom they worked. They had developed ambition, individuality, personal initiative, and a marked degree of excellence in their work. A year after their return to their own country, the deadening, nonprogressive atmosphere about them had done its work. The men had lost the desire to improve; they were again plodders, with no goal beyond the day's work. The ambition aroused by stimulating environment had sunk to sleep again.

Our Indian schools sometimes publish, side by side, photographs of the Indian youths as they come from the reservation and as they look when they are graduated—well dressed, intelligent, with the fire of ambition in their eyes. We predict great things for them; but the majority of those who go back to their tribes, after struggling awhile to keep up their new standards, gradually drop back to their old manner of living. There are, of course, many notable exceptions, but these are strong characters, able to resist the downward-dragging tendencies about them.

If you interview the great army of failures, you will find that multitudes have failed because they never got into a stimulating, encouraging environment, because their ambition was never aroused, or because they were not strong enough to rally under depressing, discouraging, or vicious surroundings. Most of the people we find in prisons and poorhouses are pitiable examples of the influence of an environment which appealed to the worst instead of to the best in them.

Whatever you do in life, make any sacrifice necessary to keep in an ambition-arousing atmosphere, an environment that will stimulate you to self-development. Keep close to people who understand you, who believe in you, who will help you to discover yourself and encourage you to make the most of yourself. This may make all the difference to you between a grand success and a mediocre existence. Stick to those who are trying to do something and to be somebody in the world—people of high aims, lofty ambition. Keep close to those who are dead-in-earnest. Ambition is contagious. You will catch the spirit that dominates in your environment. The success of those about you who are trying to climb upward will encourage and stimulate you to struggle harder if you have not done quite so well yourself.

There is a great power in a battery of individuals who are struggling for the achievement of high aims, a great magnetic force which will help you to attract the object of your ambition. It is very stimulating to be with people whose aspirations run parallel with your own. If you lack energy, if you are naturally lazy, indolent, or inclined to take it easy, you will be urged forward by the constant prodding of the more ambitious.

He who wishes to fulfil his mission must be a man of one idea, that is, of one great overmastering purpose, over shadowing all his aims, and guiding and controlling his entire life.

—**Julius Bate**

A healthful hunger for a great idea is the beauty and blessedness of life.

—**Jean Ingelow**

A profound conviction raises a man above the feeling of ridicule.

—**J. Stuart Mill**

Ideas go booming through the world louder than cannon. Thoughts are mightier than armies. Principles have achieved more victories than horsemen or chariots.

—**W.M. Paxton**

Chapter
36

THE MAN WITH AN IDEA

"What are you bothering yourselves with a knitting machine for?" asked Ari Davis, of Boston, a manufacturer of instruments "why don't you make a sewing machine?" His advice had been sought by a rich man and an inventor who had reached their wits' ends in the vain attempt to produce a device for knitting woolen goods. "I wish I could, but it can't be done." "Oh, yes it can," said Davis; "I can make one myself." "Well," the capitalist replied, "you do it, and I'll insure you an independent fortune." The words of Davis were uttered in a spirit of jest, but the novel idea found lodgment in the mind of one of the workmen who stood by, a mere youth of 20, who was thought not capable of a serious idea.

But Elias Howe was not so rattlebrained as he seemed, and the more he reflected, the more desirable such a machine appeared to him. Four years passed, and with a wife and three children to support in a great city on a salary of nine dollars a week, the lighthearted boy had become a thoughtful, plodding man. The thought of the sewing machine haunted him night and day, and he finally resolved to produce one.

After months wasted in the effort to work a needle pointed at both ends, with the eye in the middle, that should pass up and down through the cloth, suddenly the thought flashed through his mind that another stitch must be possible, and with almost insane devotion he worked night and day, until he had made a rough model of wood and wire that convinced him of ultimate success. In his mind's eye he saw his idea, but his own funds and those of his father, who had aided him more or less, were insufficient to embody it in a working machine. But help came from an old schoolmate, George Fisher, a coal and wood merchant of

Cambridge. He agreed to board Elias and his family and furnish 500 dollars, for which he was to have one-half of the patent if the machine proved to be worth patenting.

In May, 1845, the machine was completed, and in July Elias Howe sewed all the seams of two suits of woolen clothes, one for Mr. Fisher and the other for himself. The sewing outlasted the cloth. This machine, which is still preserved, will sew 300 stitches a minute, and is considered more nearly perfect than any other prominent invention at its first trial. There is not one of the millions of sewing machines now in use that does not contain some of the essential principles of this first attempt.

When it was decided to try and elevate Chicago out of the mud by raising its immense blocks up to grade, the young son of a poor mechanic, named George M. Pullman, appeared on the scene, and put in a bid for the great undertaking, and the contract was awarded to him. He not only raised the blocks, but did it in such a way that business within them was scarcely interrupted. All this time he was revolving in his mind his pet project of building a "sleeping car" which would be adopted on all railroads. He fitted up two old cars on the Chicago and Alton Road with berths, and soon found they would be in demand. He then went to work on the principle that the more luxurious his cars were, the greater would be the demand for them. After spending three years in Colorado gold mines, he returned and built two cars which cost $18,000 each. Everybody laughed at "Pullman's folly." But Pullman believed that whatever relieved the tediousness of long trips would meet with speedy approval, and he had faith enough in his idea to risk his all in it.

Pullman was a great believer in the commercial value of beauty. The wonderful town which he built and which bears his name, as well as his magnificent cars, is an example of his belief in this principle. He counts it a good investment to surround his employees with comforts and beauty and good sanitary conditions, and so the town of Pullman is a model of cleanliness, order, and comfort.

It has ever been the man with an idea, which he puts into practical effect, who has changed the face of Christendom. The germ idea of the steam engine can be seen in the writings of the Greek philosophers, but it was not developed until more than two thousand years later.

It was an English blacksmith, Newcomen, with no opportunities, who in the seventeenth century conceived the idea of moving a piston by the elastic force of steam; but his engine consumed 30 pounds of coal in producing one horsepower. The perfection of the modern engine is largely due to James Watt, a poor, uneducated Scotch boy, who at 15 walked the streets of London in a vain search for work.

A professor in Glasgow University gave him the use of a room to work in, and while waiting for jobs he experimented with old vials for steam reservoirs and hollow canes for pipes, for he could not bear to waste a moment. He improved Newcomen's engine by cutting off the steam after the piston had completed a quarter or a third of its stroke, and letting the steam already in the chamber expand and drive the piston the remaining distance. This saved nearly three-fourths of the steam. Watt suffered from pinching poverty and hardships which would have disheartened ordinary men; but he was terribly in earnest, and his brave wife Margaret begged him not to mind her inconvenience, nor be discouraged. "If the engine will not work," she wrote him while struggling in London, "something else will. Never despair."

"I had gone to take a walk," said Watt, "on a fine Sabbath afternoon, and had passed the old washing house, thinking upon the engine at the time, when the idea came into my head that, as steam is an elastic body, it would rush into a vacuum, and if a communication were made between the cylinder and an exhausted vessel, it would rush into it, and might be there condensed without cooling the cylinder." The idea was simple, but in it lay the germ of the first steam engine of much practical value. Sir James Mackintosh places this poor Scotch boy who began with only an idea "at the head of all inventors in all ages and all nations."

See George Stephenson, working in the coal pits for sixpence a day, patching the clothes and mending the boots of his fellow workmen at night, to earn a little money to attend a night school, giving the first money he ever earned, $150, to his blind father to pay his debts. People say he is crazy; his "roaring steam engine will set the house on fire with its sparks"; "smoke will pollute the air"; "carriage makers and coachmen will starve for want of work." For three days the committee of the House of Commons plies questions to him. This was one of them: "If a cow get on the track of the engine traveling 10 miles an hour, will it not be an awkward situation?" "Yes, very awkward, indeed, for the coo," replied Stephenson. A government inspector said that if a locomotive ever went 10 miles an hour, he would undertake to eat a stewed engine for breakfast.

"What can be more palpably absurd and ridiculous than the prospect held out of locomotives traveling twice as fast as horses?"

asked a writer in the English *Quarterly Review* for March, 1825. "We should as soon expect the people of Woolwich to suffer themselves to be fired off upon one of Congreve's rockets as to trust themselves to the mercy of such a machine, going at such a rate. We trust that Parliament will, in all the railways it may grant, *limit the speed to eight or nine miles an hour*, which we entirely agree with Mr. Sylvester is as great as can be ventured upon." This article referred to Stephenson's proposition to use his newly invented locomotive instead of horses on the Liverpool and Manchester Railroad, then in process of construction.

The company decided to lay the matter before two leading English engineers, who reported that steam would be desirable only when used in stationary engines one and a half miles apart, drawing the cars by means of ropes and pulleys. But Stephenson persuaded them to test his idea by offering a prize of about 2,500 dollars for the best locomotive produced at a trial to take place October 6, 1829.

On the eventful day, thousands of spectators assembled to watch the competition of four engines, the *Novelty*, the *Rocket*, the *Perseverance*, and the *Sanspareil*. The *Perseverance* could make but six miles an hour, and so was ruled out, as the conditions called for at least ten. The *Sanspareil* made an average of 14 miles an hour, but as it burst a water pipe it lost its chance. The *Novelty* did splendidly, but also burst a pipe, and was crowded out, leaving the *Rocket* to carry off the honors with an average speed of 15 miles an hour, the highest rate attained being 29. This was Stephenson's locomotive, and so fully vindicated his theory that the idea of stationary engines on a railroad was completely exploded. He had picked up the fixed engines which the genius of Watt had devised, and set them on wheels to draw men and merchandise, against the most direful predictions of the foremost engineers of his day.

In all the records of invention there is no more sad or affecting story than that of John Fitch. Poor he was in many senses, poor in appearance, poor in spirit. He was born poor, lived poor, and died poor. If there ever was a true inventor, this man was one. He was one of those eager souls that would coin their own flesh to carry their point. He only uttered the obvious truth when he said one day, in a crisis of his invention, that if he could get 100 pounds by cutting off one of his legs, he would gladly give it to the knife.

He tried in vain both in this country and in France to get money to build his steamboat. He would say: "You and I will not live to see the day, but the time will come when the steamboat will be preferred to all other modes of conveyance, when steamboats will ascend the Western rivers from New Orleans to Wheeling, and when steamboats will cross the ocean. Johnny Fitch will be forgotten, but other men will carry out his ideas and grow rich and great upon them."

Poor, ragged, forlorn, jeered at, pitied as a madman, discouraged by the great, refused by the rich, he kept on till, in 1790, he had the first vessel on the Delaware that ever answered the purpose of a steamboat. It ran six miles an hour against the tide, and eight miles with it.

At noon, on Friday, August 4, 1807, a crowd of curious people might have been seen along the wharves of the Hudson River. They had gathered to witness what they considered a ridiculous failure of a "crank" who proposed to take a party of people up the Hudson River to Albany in what he called a steam vessel named the *Clermont*. Did anybody ever hear of such a ridiculous idea as navigating against the current up the Hudson in a vessel without sails? "The thing will 'bust,'" says one; "it will burn up," says another, and "they will all be drowned," exclaims a third, as he sees vast columns of black smoke shoot up with showers of brilliant sparks.

Nobody present, in all probability, ever heard of a boat going by steam. It was the opinion of everybody that the man who had tooled away his money and his time on the *Clermont* was little better than an idiot, and ought to be in an insane asylum. But the passengers go on board, the plank is pulled in, and the steam is turned on. The walking beam moves slowly up and down, and the *Clermont* floats out into the river. "It can never go up stream," the spectators persist. But it did go up stream, and the boy, who in his youth said there is nothing impossible, had scored a great triumph, and had given to the world the first steamboat that had any practical value.

Notwithstanding that Fulton had rendered such great service to humanity, a service which has revolutionized the commerce of the world, he was looked upon by many as a public enemy. Critics and cynics turned up their noses when Fulton was mentioned. The severity of the world's censure, ridicule, and detraction has usually been in proportion to the benefit the victim has conferred upon mankind.

As the *Clermont* burned pine wood, dense columns of fire and smoke belched forth from her smokestack while she glided triumphantly up the river, and the inhabitants along the banks were utterly unable to account for the spectacle. They rushed to the shore amazed to see a boat "on fire" go against the stream so rapidly with neither oars nor sails. The noise of her great paddle wheels increased the wonder. Sailors forsook their vessels, and fishermen rowed home as fast as possible to get out of the way of the fire monster. The Indians were as much frightened as their predecessors were when the first ship approached their hunting ground on Manhattan Island.

The owners of sailing vessels were jealous of the *Clermont* and tried to run her down. Others whose interests were affected denied Fulton's claim to the invention and brought suits against him. But the success of the *Clermont* soon led to the construction of other steamships all over the country. The government employed Fulton to aid in building a powerful steam frigate, which was called Fulton the First. He also built a diving boat for the government for the discharge of torpedoes. By this time his fame had spread all over the civilized world, and when he died, in 1815, newspapers were marked with black lines; the legislature of New York wore badges of mourning; and minute guns were fired as the long funeral procession passed to old Trinity churchyard. Very few private persons were ever honored with such a burial.

True, Dr. Lardner had "proved" to scientific men that a steamship could not cross the Atlantic, but in 1819 the *Savannah* from New York appeared off the coast of Ireland under sail and steam, having made this "impossible" passage. Those on shore thought that a fire had broken out below the decks, and a king's cutter was sent to her relief. Although the voyage was made without accident, it was nearly 20 years before it was admitted that steam navigation could be made a commercial success in ocean traffic.

As Junius Smith impatiently paced the deck of a vessel sailing from an English port to New York, on a rough and tedious voyage in 1832, he said to himself, "Why not cross the ocean regularly in steamships?" In New York and in London a deaf ear was turned to any such nonsense. Smith's first encouragement came from George Grote, the historian and banker, who said the idea was practicable; but it was the same old story—he would risk no money in it. At length Isaac Selby, a prominent business man of London, agreed to build a steamship of 2,000 tons, the *British Queen*. An unexpected delay in fitting the engines led the projectors to charter the *Sirius*, a river steamer of 700 tons, and send her to New York. Learning of this, other parties started from Bristol four days later in the *Great Western*, and both vessels arrived at New York the same day. Soon after Smith made the round trip between London and New York in 32 days.

What a sublime picture of determination and patience was that of Charles Goodyear, of New Haven, buried in poverty and struggling with hardships for 11 long years, to make India rubber of practical use! See him in prison for debt; pawning his clothes and his wife's jewelry to get a little money to keep his children (who were obliged to gather sticks in the field for fire) from starving. Watch his sublime courage and devotion to his idea, when he had no money to bury a dead child and when his other five were near starvation; when his neighbors were harshly criticizing him for his neglect of his family and calling him insane. But, behold his vulcanized rubber; the result of that heroic struggle, applied to over 500 uses by 100,000 employees.

What a pathetic picture was that of Palissy, plodding on through want and woe to rediscover the lost art of enameling pottery; building his furnaces with bricks carried on his back, seeing his six children die of neglect, probably of starvation, his wife in rags and despair over her husband's "folly"; despised by his neighbors for neglecting his family, worn to a skeleton himself, giving his clothes to his hired man because he could not pay him in money, hoping always, failing steadily, until at last his great work was accomplished, and he reaped his reward.

German unity was the idea engraved upon Bismarck's heart. What cared this herculean despot for the Diet chosen year after year simply to vote down every measure he proposed? He was indifferent to all opposition. He simply defied and sent home every Diet which opposed him. He could play the game alone. To make Germany the greatest power in Europe, to make William of Prussia a greater potentate than Napoleon or Alexander, was his all-absorbing purpose. It mattered not what stood in his way, whether people, Diet, or nation; all must bend to his mighty will. Germany must hold the deciding voice in the Areopagus of the world. He rode roughshod over everybody and everything that stood in his way, defiant of opposition, imperious, irrepressible!

See the great Dante in exile, condemned to be burnt alive on false charges of embezzlement. Look at his starved features, gaunt form, melancholy, a poor wanderer; but he never gave up his idea; he poured out his very soul into his immortal poem, ever believing that right would at last triumph.

Columbus was exposed to continual scoffs and indignities, being ridiculed as a mere dreamer and stigmatized as an adventurer. The very children, it is said, pointed to their foreheads as he passed, being taught to regard him as a kind of madman.

An American was once invited to dine with Oken, the famous German naturalist. To his surprise, they had neither meats nor dessert, but only baked potatoes. Oken was too great a man to apologize for their simple fare. His wife explained, however, that her husband's income was very small, and that they preferred to live simply in order that he might obtain books and instruments for his scientific researches.

Before the discovery of ether, it often took a week, in some cases a month, to recover from the enormous dose, sometimes 500 drops of laudanum, given to a patient to deaden the pain during a surgical operation. Young Dr. Morton believed that there must be some means provided by Nature to relieve human suffering during these terrible operations; but what could he do? He was not a chemist; he did not know the properties of chemical substances; he was not liberally educated.

Dr. Morton did not resort to books, however, nor did he go to scientific men for advice, but immediately began to experiment with well-known substances. He tried intoxicants even to the point of intoxication, but as soon as the instruments were applied the patient would revive. He kept on experimenting with narcotics in this manner until at last he found what he sought in ether.

What a grand idea Bishop Vincent worked out for the young world in the Chautauqua Circle, Dr. Clark in his worldwide Christian Endeavor movement, the Methodist Church in the Epworth League, Edward Everett Hale in his little bands of King's Daughters and Ten Times One is Ten! Here is Clara Barton who has created the Red Cross Society, which is loved by all nations. She noticed in our Civil War that the Confederates were shelling the hospital. She thought it the last touch of cruelty to fight what couldn't fight back, and she determined to have the barbarous custom stopped. Of course, the world laughed at this poor unaided woman. But her idea has been adopted by all nations; and the enemy that aims a shot at the tent or building over which flies the white flag with the red cross has lost his last claim to human consideration.

In all ages those who have advanced the cause of humanity have been men and women "possessed," in the opinion of their neighbors. Noah in building the ark, Moses in espousing the cause of the Israelites, or Christ in living and dying to save a fallen race, incurred the pity and scorn of the rich and highly educated, in common with all great benefactors. Yet in every age and in every clime men and women have been willing to incur poverty, hardship, toil, ridicule, persecution, or even death, if thereby they might shed light or comfort upon the path which all must walk from the cradle to the grave. In fact, it is doubtful whether a man can perform very great service to mankind who is not permeated with a great purpose—with an overmastering idea.

Beecher had to fight every step of the way to his triumph through obstacles which would have appalled all but the greatest characters. Oftentimes in these great battles for principle and struggles for truth, he stood almost alone fighting popular prejudice, narrowness, and bigotry, uncharitableness and envy even in his own church. But he never hesitated nor wavered when he once saw his duty. There was no shilly-shallying, no hunting for a middle ground between right and wrong, no compromise on principles. He hewed close to the chalk line and held his line plumb to truth. He never pandered for public favor nor sought applause. Duty and truth were his goal, and he went straight to his mark. Other churches did not agree with him nor his, but he was too broad for hatred, too charitable for revenge, and too magnanimous for envy.

What tale of the *Arabian Nights* equals in fascination the story of such lives as those of Franklin, of Morse, Goodyear, Howe, Edison, Bell, Beecher, Gough, Mrs. Harriet Beecher Stowe, Amos Lawrence, George Peabody, McCormick, Hoe, and scores of others, each representing some great idea embodied in earnest action, and resulting in an improvement of the physical, mental, and moral condition of those around them?

There are plenty of ideas left in the world yet. Everything has not been invented. All good things have not been done. There are thousands of abuses to rectify, and each one challenges the independent soul, armed with a new idea.

"But how shall I get ideas?" Keep your wits open! Observe! Study! But above all, think! and when a noble image is indelibly impressed upon the mind—act!

The Spartans did not inquire how many the enemy are, but where they are.

—*Agis II*

What's brave, what's noble, let's do it after the high Roman fashion, and make death proud to take us.

—**William Shakespeare**

Let me die facing the enemy.

—**Chevalier de Bayard**

Who conquers me, shall find a stubborn foe.

—**Lord Byron**

*No great deed is done
By falterers who ask for certainty.*

—**George Eliot**

To stand with a smile upon your face against a stake from which you cannot get away—that, no doubt, is heroic. But the true glory is resignation to the inevitable. To stand unchained, with perfect liberty to go away, held only by the higher claims of duty, and let the fire creep up to the heart—this is heroism.

—*F.W. Robertson*

Fortune befriends the bold.

—*Virgil*

Chapter 37

DARE

"Steady, men! Every man must die where he stands!" said Colin Campbell to the Ninety-third Highlanders at Balaklava, as an overwhelming force of Russian cavalry came sweeping down. "Ay, ay, Sir Colin! we'll do that!" was the response from men, many of whom had to keep their word by thus obeying.

"Bring back the colors," shouted a captain at the battle of the Alma, when an ensign maintained his ground in front, although the men were retreating. "No," cried the ensign, "bring up the men to the colors."

"To dare, and again to dare, and without end to dare," was Danton's noble defiance to the enemies of France. "The Commons of France have resolved to deliberate," said Mirabeau to De Breze, who brought an order from the king for them to disperse, June 23, 1789. "We have heard the intentions that have been attributed to the king; and you, sir, who cannot be recognized as his organ in the National Assembly— you, who have neither place, voice, nor right to speak—you are not the person to bring to us a message of his. Go, say to those who sent you that we are here by the power of the people, and that we will not be driven hence, save by the power of the bayonet."

When the assembled senate of Rome begged Regulus not to return to Carthage to fulfil an illegal promise, he calmly replied: "Have you resolved to dishonor me? Torture and death are awaiting me, but what are these to the shame of an infamous act, or the wounds of a guilty mind? Slave as I am to Carthage, I still have the spirit of a Roman. I have sworn to return. It is my duty. Let the gods take care of the rest."

The courage which Cranmer had shown since the accession of Mary gave way the moment his final doom was announced. The moral cowardice which had displayed itself in his miserable compliance with the lust and despotism of Henry VIII displayed itself again in six successive recantations by which he hoped to purchase pardon. But pardon was impossible; and Cranmer's strangely mingled nature found a power in its very weakness when he was brought into the church of St. Mary at Oxford on the 21st of March, to repeat his recantation on the way to the stake. "Now," ended his address to the hushed congregation before him, "now I come to the great thing that troubled my conscience more than any other thing that ever I said or did in my life, and that is the setting abroad of writings contrary to the truth; which here I now renounce and refuse as things written by a hand contrary to the truth which I thought in my heart, and written for fear of death, to save my life, if it might be. And, forasmuch as my hand offended in writing contrary to my heart, my hand therefore shall be the first punished; for if I come to the fire, it shall be the first burned." "This was the hand that wrote it," he again exclaimed at the stake, "therefore it shall suffer first punishment"; and holding it steadily in the flame, "he never stirred nor cried till life was gone."

A woman's piercing shriek suddenly startled a party of surveyors at dinner in a forest of northern Virginia on a calm, sunny day in 1750. The cries were repeated in quick succession, and the men sprang through the undergrowth to learn their cause. "Oh, sir," exclaimed the woman as she caught sight of a youth of 18, but a man in stature and bearing; "you will surely do something for me! Make these friends release me. My boy, my poor boy is drowning, and they will not let me go!" "It would be madness; she will jump into the river," said one of the men who was holding her; "and the rapids would dash her to pieces in a moment!" Throwing off his coat, the youth sprang to the edge of the bank, scanned for a moment the rocks and whirling currents, and then, at sight of part of the boy's dress, plunged into the roaring rapids. "Thank God, he will save my child!" cried the mother, and all rushed to the brink of the precipice; "there he is! Oh, my boy, my darling boy! How could I leave you?"

But all eyes were bent upon the youth struggling with strong heart and hope amid the dizzy sweep of the whirling currents far below. Now it seemed as if he would be dashed against a projecting rock, over which the water flew in foam, and anon a whirlpool would drag him in, from whose grasp escape would seem impossible. Twice the boy went out of sight, but he had reappeared the second time, although terribly near the most dangerous part of the river. The rush of waters here was tremendous, and no one had ever dared to approach it, even in a canoe, lest he should be dashed to pieces. The youth redoubled his exertions. Three times he was about to grasp the child, when some stronger eddy would toss it from him. One final effort he makes; the child is held aloft by his strong right arm; but a cry of horror bursts from the lips of every spectator as boy and man shoot over the falls and vanish in the seething waters below.

"There they are!" shouted the mother a moment later, in a delirium of joy. "See! they are safe! Great God, I thank Thee!" And sure enough, they emerged unharmed from the boiling vortex, and in a few minutes reached a low place in the bank and were drawn up by their friends, the boy senseless, but still alive, and the youth almost exhausted. "God will give you a reward," solemnly spoke the grateful woman. "He will do great things for you in return for this day's work, and the blessings of thousands besides mine will attend you."

The youth was George Washington.

"Your Grace has not the organ of animal courage largely developed," said a phrenologist, who was examining Wellington's head. "You are right," replied the Iron Duke, "and but for my sense of duty I should have retreated in my first fight." That first fight, on an Indian field, was one of the most terrible on record.

When General Jackson was a judge and was holding court in a small settlement, a border ruffian, a murderer and desperado, came into the courtroom with brutal violence and interrupted the court. The judge ordered him to be arrested. The officer did not dare to approach him. "Call a posse," said the judge, "and arrest him." But they also shrank in fear from the ruffian. "Call me, then," said Jackson; "this court is adjourned for five minutes." He left the bench, walked straight up to the man, and with his eagle eye actually cowed the ruffian, who dropped his weapons, afterwards saying, "There was something in his eye I could not resist."

One of the last official acts of President Carnot, of France, was the sending of a medal of the French Legion of Honor to a little American girl who lives in Indiana. While a train on the Pan Handle Railroad, having on board several distinguished Frenchmen, was bound to Chicago and the World's Fair, Jennie Carey, who was then 10 years old, discovered that a trestle was on fire, and that if the train, which was nearly due, entered it a dreadful wreck would take place. Thereupon she ran out upon the track to a place where she could be seen from some little distance. Then she took off her red flannel skirt and, when the train came in view, waved it back and forth across the track. It was seen, and the train stopped. On board of it were 700 people, many of whom must have suffered death but for Jennie's courage and presence of mind. When they returned to France, the Frenchmen brought the occurrence to the notice of President Carnot, and the result was the sending of the medal of this famous French society, the purpose of which is the honoring of bravery and merit, wherever they may be found.

It was the heroic devotion of an Indian girl that saved the life of Captain John Smith, when the powerful King Powhatan had decreed his death. Ill could the struggling colony spare him at that time.

On May 10, 1796, Napoleon carried the bridge at Lodi, in the face of the Austrian batteries. Fourteen cannons—some accounts say thirty—were trained upon the French end of the structure. Behind them were 6,000 troops. Napoleon massed 4,000 grenadiers at the head of the bridge, with a battalion of 300 carbineers in front. At the tap of the drum the foremost assailants wheeled from the cover of the street wall under a terrible hail of grape and canister, and attempted to pass the gateway to the bridge. The front ranks went down like stalks of grain before a reaper; the column staggered and reeled backward, and the valiant grenadiers were appalled by the task before them. Without a word or a look of reproach, Napoleon placed himself at their head, and his aides and generals rushed to his side. Forward again, this time over heaps of dead that choked the passage, and a quick run, counted by seconds only, carried the column across 200 yards of clear space, scarcely a shot from the Austrians taking effect beyond the point where the platoons wheeled for the first leap. So sudden and so miraculous was it all that the Austrian artillerists abandoned their guns instantly, and instead of rushing to the front and meeting the French onslaught, their supports fled in a panic. This Napoleon had counted on in making the bold attack. The contrast between Napoleon's slight figure and the massive grenadiers suggested the nickname "Little Corporal."

When Stephen of Colonna fell into the hands of base assailants, they asked him in derision, "Where is now your fortress?" "Here," was his bold reply, placing his hand upon his heart.

After the Mexican War General McClellan was employed as

a topographical engineer in surveying the Pacific coast. From his headquarters at Vancouver, he had gone on an exploring expedition with two companions, a soldier and a servant, when one evening he received word that the chiefs of the Columbia River tribes desired to confer with him. From the messenger's manner he suspected that the Indians meant mischief, and so he warned his companions that they must be ready to leave camp at a moment's notice.

Mounting his horse, he rode boldly into the Indian village. About 30 chiefs were holding council. McClellan was led into the circle, and placed at the right hand of Saltese. He was familiar with the Chinook jargon, and could understand every word spoken in the council. Saltese made known the grievance of the tribes. Two Indians had been captured by a party of white pioneers and hanged for theft. Retaliation for this outrage seemed imperative. The chiefs pondered long, but had little to say. McClellan had been on friendly terms with them, and was not responsible for the forest executions, but still, he was a white man, and the chiefs had vowed vengeance against the race. The council was prolonged for hours before sentence was passed, and then Saltese, in the name of the head men of the tribes, decreed that McClellan should immediately be put to death.

McClellan said nothing. He had known that argument and pleas for justice or mercy would be of no avail. He sat motionless, apparently indifferent to his fate. By his listlessness he had thrown his captors off their guard. When the sentence was passed, he acted like a flash. Flinging his left arm around the neck of Saltese, he whipped out his revolver and held it close to the chief's temple. "Revoke that sentence, or I shall kill you this instant!" he cried, with his fingers clicking the trigger. "I revoke it!" exclaimed Saltese, fairly livid from fear. "I must have your word that I can leave this council in safety." "You have the word of Saltese," was the quick response.

McClellan knew how sacred was the pledge which he had received. The revolver was lowered. Saltese was released from the embrace of the strong arm. McClellan strode out of the tent with his revolver in his hand. Not a hand was raised against him. He mounted his horse and rode to his camp, where his two followers were ready to spring into the saddle and to escape from the villages. He owed his life to his quickness of perception, his courage, and to his accurate knowledge of Indian character.

In 1856, Rufus Choate spoke to an audience of nearly 5,000 in

Lowell, Mass., in favor of the candidacy of James Buchanan for the presidency. The floor of the great hall began to sink, settling more and more as he proceeded with his address, until a sound of cracking timber below would have precipitated a stampede with fatal results but for the coolness of B. F. Butler, who presided. Telling the people to remain quiet, he said that he would see if there were any cause for alarm. He found the supports of the floor in so bad a condition that the slightest applause would be likely to bury the audience in the ruins of the building. Returning rather leisurely to the platform, he whispered to Choate as he passed, "We shall all be in—in five minutes"; then he told the crowd that there was no immediate danger if they would slowly disperse. The post of danger, he added, was on the platform, which was most weakly supported, therefore he and those with him would be the last to leave. No doubt many lives were saved by his coolness.

Many distinguished foreign and American statesmen were present at a fashionable dinner party where wine was freely poured, but Schuyler Colfax, then vice president of the United States, declined to drink from a proffered cup. "Colfax dares not drink," sneered a Senator who had already taken too much. "You are right," said the Vice President, "I dare not."

When Grant was in Houston many years ago, he was given a rousing reception. Naturally hospitable, and naturally inclined to like a man of Grant's makeup, the Houstonites determined to go beyond any other Southern city in the way of a banquet and other manifestations of their goodwill and hospitality. They made lavish preparations for the dinner, the committee taking great pains to have the finest wines that could be procured for the table that night. When the time came to serve the wine, the headwaiter went first to Grant. Without a word the general quietly turned down all the glasses at his plate. This movement was a great surprise to the Texans, but they were equal to the occasion. Without a single word being spoken, every man along the line of the long tables turned his glasses down, and there was not a drop of wine taken that night.

Two French officers at Waterloo were advancing to charge a greatly superior force. One, observing that the other showed signs of fear, said, "Sir, I believe you are frightened." "Yes, I am," was the reply, "and if you were half as much frightened, you would run away."

"That's a brave man," said Wellington, when he saw a soldier turn pale as he marched against a battery; "he knows his danger, and faces it."

"There are many cardinals and bishops at Worms," said a friend to Luther, "and they will burn your body to ashes as they did that of John Huss." Luther replied: "Although they should make a fire that should reach from Worms to Wittenberg, and that should flame up to heaven, in the Lord's name I would pass through it and appear before them." He said to another: "I would enter Worms though there were as many devils there as there are tiles upon the roofs of the houses." Another man said to him: "Duke George will surely arrest you." He replied: "It is my duty to go, and I will go, though it rains Duke Georges for nine days together."

A Western paper recently invited the surviving Union and Confederate officers to give an account of the bravest act observed by each during the Civil War. Colonel Thomas Wentworth Higginson said that at a dinner at Beaufort, S. C., where wine flowed freely and ribald jests were bandied, Dr. Miner, a slight, boyish fellow who did not drink, was told that he could not go until he had drunk a toast, told a story, or sung a song. He replied: "I cannot sing, but I will give a toast, although I must drink it in water. It is 'Our Mothers.'" The men were so affected and ashamed that they took him by the hand and thanked him for displaying such admirable moral courage.

It takes courage for a young man to stand firmly erect while others are bowing and fawning for praise and power. It takes courage to wear threadbare clothes while your comrades dress in broadcloth. It takes courage to remain in honest poverty when others grow rich by fraud. It takes courage to say "No" squarely when those around you say "Yes." It takes courage to do your duty in silence and obscurity while others prosper and grow famous although neglecting sacred obligations. It takes courage to unmask your true self, to show your blemishes to a condemning world, and to pass for what you really are.

It takes courage and pluck to be outvoted, beaten, laughed at, scoffed, ridiculed, derided, misunderstood, misjudged, to stand alone with all the world against you, but

> *They are slaves who dare not be*
> *In the right with two or three.*

> *An honest man is not the worse because a dog barks at him.*
> *We live ridiculously for fear of being thought ridiculous.*
> *Tis he is the coward who proves false to his vows,*
> *To his manhood, his honor, for a laugh or a sneer.*

The youth who starts out by being afraid to speak what he thinks will usually end by being afraid to think what he wishes.

How we shrink from an act of our own! We live as others live. Custom or fashion, or your doctor or minister, dictates, and they in turn dare not depart from their schools. Dress, living, servants, carriages, everything must conform, or we are ostracized. Who dares conduct his household or business affairs in his own way, and snap his fingers at Dame Grundy?

It takes courage for a public man not to bend the knee to popular prejudice. It takes courage to refuse to follow custom when it is injurious to his health and morals. How much easier for a politician to prevaricate and dodge an issue than to stand squarely on his feet like a man!

As the strongest man has a weakness somewhere, so the greatest hero is a coward somewhere. Peter was courageous enough to draw his sword to defend his Master, but he could not stand the ridicule and the finger of scorn of the maidens in the high priest's hall, and he actually denied even the acquaintance of the Master he had declared he would die for.

Don't be like Uriah Heep, begging everybody's pardon for taking the liberty of being in the world. There is nothing attractive in timidity, nothing lovable in fear. Both are deformities and are repulsive. Manly courage is always dignified and graceful.

Giordano Bruno, condemned to be burned alive in Rome, said to his judge: "You are more afraid to pronounce my sentence than I am to receive it." Anne Askew, racked until her bones were dislocated, never flinched, but looked her tormentor calmly in the face and refused to adjure her faith.

"I should have thought fear would have kept you from going so far," said a relative who found the little boy Nelson wandering a long distance from home. "Fear?" said the future admiral, "I don't know him."

"To think a thing is impossible is to make it so." Courage is victory, timidity's defeat.

That simple shepherd lad, David, fresh from his flocks, marching unattended and unarmed, save with his shepherd's staff and sling, to confront the colossal Goliath with his massive armor, is the sublimest audacity the world has ever seen.

"Dent, I wish you would get down and see what is the matter with that leg there," said Grant, when he and Colonel Dent were riding through the thickest of a fire that had become so concentrated and murderous that his troops had all been driven back. "I guess looking after your horse's legs can wait," said Dent; "it is simply murder for us to sit here." "All right," said Grant; "if you don't want to see to it, I will." He dismounted, untwisted a piece of telegraph wire which had begun to cut the horse's leg, examined it deliberately, and climbed into his saddle. "Dent," said he, "when you've got a horse that you think a great deal of, you should never take any chances with him. If that wire had been left there for a little time longer, he would have gone dead lame, and would perhaps have been ruined for life."

Wellington said that at Waterloo the hottest of the battle raged round a farmhouse, with an orchard surrounded by a thick hedge, which was so important a point in the British position that orders were given to hold it at any hazard or sacrifice. At last, the powder and ball ran short and the hedges took fire, surrounding the orchard with a wall of flame. A messenger had been sent for ammunition, and soon two loaded wagons came galloping toward the farmhouse. "The driver of the first wagon, with the reckless daring of an English boy, spurred his struggling and terrified horses through the burning heap; but the flames rose fiercely round, and caught the powder, which exploded in an instant, sending wagon, horses, and rider in fragments into the air. For an instant the driver of the second wagon paused, appalled by his comrade's fate; the next, observing that the flames, beaten back for the moment by the explosion, afforded him one desperate chance, sent his horses at the smoldering breach and, amid the deafening cheers of the garrison, landed his terrible cargo safely within. Behind him the flames closed up, and raged more fiercely than ever."

At the battle of Friedland a cannon ball came over the heads of the French soldiers, and a young soldier instinctively dodged. Napoleon looked at him and smilingly said: "My friend, if that ball were destined for you, though you were to burrow a hundred feet underground it would be sure to find you there."

When the mine in front of Petersburg was finished the fuse was lighted and the Union troops were drawn up ready to charge the enemy's works as soon as the explosion should make a breach. But seconds, minutes, and tens of minutes passed, without a sound from the mine, and the suspense became painful. Lieutenant Doughty and Sergeant Rees volunteered to examine the fuse. Through the long subterranean galleries, they hurried in silence, not knowing but that they were advancing to a horrible death. They found the defect, fired the train anew, and soon a terrible upheaval of earth gave the signal to march to victory.

At the battle of Copenhagen, as Nelson walked the deck slippery with blood and covered with the dead, he said: "This is warm work, and this day may be the last to any of us in a moment. But, mark me, I would not be elsewhere for thousands." At the battle of Trafalgar, when he was shot and was being carried below, he covered his face, that those fighting might not know their chief had fallen.

In a skirmish at Salamanca, while the enemy's guns were pouring shot into his regiment, Sir William Napier's men became disobedient. He at once ordered a halt, and flogged four of the ringleaders under fire. The men yielded at once, and then marched three miles under a heavy cannonade as coolly as if it were a review.

Execute your resolutions immediately. Thoughts are but dreams until their effects be tried. Does competition trouble you? work away; what is your competitor but a man? Conquer your place in the world, for all things serve a brave soul. Combat difficulty manfully; sustain misfortune bravely; endure poverty nobly; encounter disappointment courageously. The influence of the brave man is contagious and creates an epidemic of noble zeal in all about him. Every day sends to the grave obscure men who have only remained in obscurity because their timidity has prevented them from making a first effort; and who, if they could have been induced to begin, would in all probability have gone great lengths in the career of usefulness and fame. "No great deed is done," says George Eliot, "by falterers who ask for certainty."

After the great inward struggle was over, and he had determined to remain loyal to his principles, Thomas More walked cheerfully to the block. His wife called him a fool for staying in a dark, damp, filthy prison when he might have his liberty by merely renouncing his doctrines, as some of the bishops had done. But Thomas More preferred death to dishonor.

His daughter showed the power of love to drive away fear. She remained true to her father when all others, even her mother, had forsaken him. After his head had been cut off and exhibited on a pole on London Bridge, the poor girl begged it of the authorities, and requested that it be buried in the coffin with her. Her request was granted, for her death soon occurred.

When Sir Walter Raleigh came to the scaffold, he was very faint, and began his speech to the crowd by saying that during the last two days he had been visited by two ague fits. "If, therefore, you perceive any weakness in me, I beseech you ascribe it to my sickness rather than

to myself." He took the ax and kissed the blade and said to the ,
"It is a sharp medicine, but a sound cure for all diseases."

Don't waste time dreaming of obstacles you may never encounter,
or in crossing bridges you have not reached. To half will and to hang
forever in the balance is to lose your grip on life.

Abraham Lincoln's boyhood was one long struggle with poverty,
with little education, and no influential friends. When at last he had begun
the practice of law, it required no little courage to cast his fortune with
the weaker side in politics, and thus imperil what small reputation he had
gained. Only the most sublime moral courage could have sustained him
as President to hold his ground against hostile criticism and a long train
of disaster; to issue the Emancipation Proclamation, to support Grant
and Stanton against the clamor of the politicians and the press.

Lincoln never shrank from espousing an unpopular cause when he
believed it to be right. At the time when it almost cost a young lawyer
his bread and butter to defend the fugitive slave, and when other lawyers
had refused, Lincoln would always plead the cause of the unfortunate
whenever an opportunity presented. "Go to Lincoln," people would say,
when these hounded fugitives were seeking protection; "he's not afraid
of any cause, if it's right."

> *Then to side with Truth is noble when we share her*
> *wretched crust, ere her cause brings fame and profit, and*
> *'tis prosperous to be just: Then it is the brave man chooses,*
> *while the coward stands aside, doubting in his abject*
> *spirit, till his Lord is crucified.*
> **—James Russell Lowell**

As Salmon P. Chase left the court room after an impassioned plea
for the runaway slave girl Matilda, a man looked at him in surprise and
said: "There goes a fine young fellow who has just ruined himself." But
in thus ruining himself Chase had taken the first important step in a
career in which he became Governor of Ohio, United States Senator
from Ohio, Secretary of the United States Treasury, and Chief Justice
of the United States Supreme Court.

At the trial of William Penn for having spoken at a Quaker meeting,
the recorder, not satisfied with the first verdict, said to the jury: "We
will have a verdict by the help of God, or you shall starve for it." "You
are Englishmen," said Penn; "mind your privileges, give not away your

right." At last, the jury, after two days and two nights without food, returned a verdict of "Not guilty." The recorder fined them 40 marks apiece for their independence.

What cared Christ for the jeers of the crowd? The palsied hand moved, the blind saw, the leper was made whole, the dead spoke, despite the ridicule and scoffs of the spectators.

What cared Wendell Phillips for rotten eggs, derisive scorn, and hisses? In him "at last the scornful world had met its match." Were Beecher and Gough to be silenced by the rude English mobs that came to extinguish them? No! they held their ground and compelled unwilling thousands to hear and to heed. Did Anna Dickinson leave the platform when the pistol bullets of the Molly Maguires flew about her head? She silenced those pistols by her courage and her arguments.

What the world wants is a Knox, who dares to preach on with a musket leveled at his head; a Garrison, who is not afraid of a jail, or a mob, or a scaffold erected in front of his door.

When General Butler was sent with 9,000 men to quell the New York riots, he arrived in advance of his troops, and found the streets thronged with an angry mob, which had already hanged several men to lampposts. Without waiting for his men, Butler went to the place where the crowd was most dense, overturned an ash barrel, stood upon it, and began: "Delegates from Five Points, fiends from hell, you have murdered your superiors," and the bloodstained crowd quailed before the courageous words of a single man in a city which Mayor Fernando Wood could not restrain with the aid of police and militia.

"Our enemies are before us," exclaimed the Spartans at Thermopylae. "And we are before them." was the cool reply of Leonidas. "Deliver your arms," came the message from Xerxes. "Come and take them," was the answer Leonidas sent back. A Persian soldier said: "You will not be able to see the sun for flying javelins and arrows." "Then we will fight in the shade," replied a Lacedemonian. What wonder that a handful of such men checked the march of the greatest host that ever trod the earth!

"It is impossible," said a staff officer, when Napoleon gave directions for a daring plan. "Impossible!" thundered the great commander, "impossible is the adjective of fools!"

The courageous man is an example to the intrepid. His influence is magnetic. Men follow him, even to the death.

Men who have dared have moved the world, often before reaching the prime of life. It is astonishing what daring to begin and perseverance have enabled even youths to achieve. Alexander, who ascended the throne at 20, had conquered the known world before dying at 33. Julius Caesar captured 800 cities, conquered 300 nations, defeated three million men, became a great orator and one of the greatest statesmen known, and still was a young man. Washington was appointed adjutant-general at 19, was sent at 21 as an ambassador to treat with the French, and won his first battle as a colonel at 22. Lafayette was made general of the whole French Army at 20. Charlemagne was master of France and Germany at 30. Galileo was but 18 when he saw the principle of the pendulum in the swing lamp in the cathedral at Pisa. Peel was in Parliament at 21. Gladstone was in Parliament before he was 22, and at 22 he was Lord of the Treasury.

Likewise, Elizabeth Barrett Browning was proficient in Greek and Latin at 12; De Quincey at 11. Robert Browning wrote at 11 poetry of no mean order. Cowley, who sleeps in Westminster Abbey, published a volume of poems at 15. Luther was but 29 when he nailed his famous thesis to the door of the bishop and defied the pope. Nelson was a lieutenant in the British Navy before he was 20. He was but 47 when he received his death wound at Trafalgar. At 36, Cortez was the conqueror of Mexico; at 32, Clive had established the British power in India. Hannibal, the greatest of military commanders, was only 30 when, at Cannae, he dealt an almost annihilating blow at the republic of Rome, and Napoleon was only 27 when, on the plains of Italy, he outgeneraled and defeated, one after another, the veteran marshals of Austria.

Equal courage and resolution are often shown by men who have passed the allotted limit of life. Victor Hugo and Wellington were both in their prime after they had reached the age of 70 years. Gladstone ruled England with a strong hand at 84, and was a marvel of literary and scholarly ability.

Shakespeare says: "He is not worthy of the honeycomb that shuns the hive because the bees have stings."

The brave man is not he who feels no fear,
For that were stupid and irrational;
But he whose noble soul its fear subdues
And bravely dares the danger nature shrinks from.

Whatever people may think of you, do that which you believe to be right. Be alike indifferent to censure or praise.

—Pythagoras

I dare to do all that may become a man: Who dares do more is none.

—William Shakespeare

For man's great actions are performed in minor struggles. There are obstinate and unknown braves who defend themselves inch by inch in the shadows against the fatal invasion of want and turpitude. There are noble and mysterious triumphs which no eye sees, no renown rewards, and no flourish of trumpets salutes. Life, misfortune, isolation, abandonment, and poverty are battlefields which have their heroes.

—Victor Hugo

Quit yourselves like men.

—1 Samuel 4:9

"I will find a way or make one."
Nothing is impossible to the man who can will.

—Honoré de Mirabeau

The iron will of one stout heart shall make a thousand quail: A feeble dwarf, dauntlessly resolved, will turn the tide of battle, And rally to a nobler strife the giants that had fled.

—Martin Tupper

In the lexicon of youth which fate reserves for a bright manhood there is no such word as fail.

—Edward Bulwer-Lytton

When a firm and decisive spirit is recognized, it is curious to see how the space clears around a man and leaves him room and freedom.

—John Foster

Chapter
38

THE WILL AND THE WAY

"As well can the Prince of Orange pluck the stars from the sky, as bring the ocean to the wall of Leyden for your relief," was the derisive shout of the Spanish soldiers when told that the Dutch fleet would raise that terrible four months' siege of 1574. But from the parched lips of William, tossing on his bed of fever at Rotterdam, had issued the command: "Break down the dikes: give Holland back to ocean!" and the people had replied: "Better a drowned land than a lost land." They began to demolish dike after dike of the strong lines, ranged one within another for 15 miles to their city of the interior. It was an enormous task; the garrison was starving; and the besiegers laughed in scorn at the slow progress of the puny insects who sought to rule the waves of the sea. But ever, as of old, Heaven aids those who help themselves.

On the first and second of October a violent equinoctial gale rolled the ocean inland, and swept the fleet on the rising waters almost to the camp of the Spaniards. The next morning the garrison sallied out to attack their enemies, but the besiegers had fled in terror under cover of the darkness. The next day the wind changed, and a counter tempest brushed the water, with the fleet upon it, from the surface of Holland. The outer dikes were replaced at once, leaving the North Sea within its old bounds. When the flowers bloomed the following spring, a joyous procession marched through the streets to found the University of Leyden, in commemoration of the wonderful deliverance of the city.

At a dinner party given in 1837, at the residence of Chancellor Kent, in New York City, some of the most distinguished men in the country were invited, and among them was a young and rather melancholy and reticent Frenchman. Professor Morse was also one of the guests, and during the evening he drew the attention of Mr. Gallatin, then a prominent statesman, to the stranger, observing that his forehead indicated a great intellect. "Yes," replied Mr. Gallatin, touching his own forehead with his finger, "there is a great deal in that head of his: but he has a strange fancy. Can you believe it? He has the idea that he will one day be the Emperor of France. Can you conceive anything more absurd than that?"

It did seem absurd, for this reserved Frenchman was then a poor adventurer, an exile from his country, without fortune or powerful connections, and yet, 14 years later, his idea became a fact—his dream of becoming Napoleon III was realized. True, before he accomplished his purpose there were long, dreary years of imprisonment, exile, disaster, and patient labor and hope, but he gained his ambition at last. He was not scrupulous as to the means employed to accomplish his ends, yet he is a remarkable example of what pluck and energy can do.

When Mr. Ingram, publisher of the *Illustrated London News*, began life as a newsdealer at Nottingham, England, he walked 10 miles to deliver a single paper rather than disappoint a customer. Does anyone wonder that such a youth succeeded? Once he rose at two o'clock in the morning and walked to London to get some papers because there was no post to bring them. He determined that his customers should not be disappointed. This is the kind of will that finds a way.

There is scarcely anything in all biography grander than the saying of young Henry Fawcett, Gladstone's last Postmaster General, to his grief-stricken father, who had put out both his eyes by birdshot during a game hunt: "Never mind, father, blindness shall not interfere with my success in life." One of the most pathetic sights in London streets, long afterward, was Henry Fawcett, MP, led everywhere by a faithful daughter, who acted as amanuensis as well as guide to her plucky father. Think of a young man, scarcely on the threshold of active life, suddenly losing the sight of both eyes and yet by mere pluck and almost incomprehensible tenacity of purpose, lifting himself into eminence in any direction, to say nothing of becoming one of the foremost men in a country noted for its great men!

The courageous daughter who was eyes to her father was herself a marvelous example of pluck and determination. For the first time in the history of Oxford College, which reaches back centuries, she succeeded in winning the post which had only been gained before by great men, such as Gladstone—the post of senior wrangler. This achievement had had no parallel in history up to that date, and attracted the attention of the whole civilized world. Not only had no woman ever held this position before, but with few exceptions it had only been held by men who in after life became highly distinguished.

"Circumstances," says Milton, "have rarely favored famous men. They have fought their way to triumph through all sorts of opposing obstacles."

The true way to conquer circumstances is to be a greater circumstance yourself.

Yet, while desiring to impress in the most forcible manner possible the fact that willpower is necessary to success, and that, other things being equal, the greater the willpower, the grander and more complete the success, we cannot endorse the theory that there is nothing in circumstances or environments, or that any man, simply because he has an indomitable will, may become a Bonaparte, a Pitt, a Webster, a Beecher, a Lincoln. We must temper determination with discretion, and support it with knowledge and common sense, or it will only lead us to run our heads against posts.

We must not expect to overcome a stubborn fact merely by a stubborn will. We only have the right to assume that we can do anything within the limit of our utmost faculty, strength, and endurance. Obstacles permanently insurmountable bar our progress in some directions, but in any direction, we may reasonably hope and attempt to go we shall find that, as a rule, they are either not insurmountable or else not permanent. The strong-willed, intelligent, persistent man will find or make a way where, in the nature of things, a way can be found or made.

Every schoolboy knows that circumstances do give clients to lawyers and patients to physicians; place ordinary clergymen in extraordinary pulpits; place sons of the rich at the head of immense corporations and large houses, when they have very ordinary ability and scarcely any experience, while poor young men with unusual ability, good education, good character, and large experience, often have to fight their way for years to obtain even very mediocre situations; that there are thousands of young men of superior ability, both in the city and in the country, who seem to be compelled by circumstances to remain in very ordinary positions for small pay, when others about them are raised by money or family influence into desirable places. In other words, we all know that the best men do not always get the best places; circumstances do have a great deal to do with our position, our salaries, our station in life.

Everyone knows that there is not always a way where there is a will; that labor does not always conquer all things; that there are things impossible even to him that wills, however strongly; that one cannot always make anything of himself he chooses; that there are limitations in our very natures which no amount of willpower or industry can overcome.

But while it is true that the willpower cannot perform miracles, yet that it is almost omnipotent, and can perform wonders, all history goes to prove. As Shakespeare says:

> *Men at some time are masters of their fates;*
> *The fault, dear Brutus, is not in our stars,*
> *But in ourselves, that we are underlings.*

Show me a man who according to popular prejudice is a victim of bad luck, and I will show you one who has some unfortunate crooked twist of temperament that invites disaster. He is ill-tempered, conceited, or trifling; lacks character, enthusiasm, or some other requisite for success.

Disraeli said that man is not the creature of circumstances, but that circumstances are the creatures of men.

Believe in the power of will, which annihilates the sickly, sentimental doctrine of fatalism—you must, but can't, you ought, but it is impossible.

Give me the man who faces what he must,

> *Who breaks his birth's invidious bar,*

> *And grasps the skirts of happy chance,*

> *And breasts the blows of circumstance,*

> *And grapples with his evil star.*

The indomitable will, the inflexible purpose, will find a way or make one. There is always room for a man of force.

"He who has a firm will," says Goethe, "molds the world to himself." "People do not lack strength," says Victor Hugo, "they lack will."

"He who resolves upon any great end, by that very resolution has scaled the great barriers to it, and he who seizes the grand idea of self-cultivation, and solemnly resolves upon it, will find that idea, that resolution, burning like fire within him, and ever putting him upon his own improvement. He will find it removing difficulties, searching out, or making means; giving courage for despondency, and strength for weakness."

Nearly all great men, those who have towered high above their fellows, have been remarkable above all things else for their energy of will. Of Julius Caesar it was said by a contemporary that it was his activity and giant determination, rather than his military skill, that won his victories. The youth who starts out in life determined to make the most of his eyes and let nothing escape him which he can possibly use for his own advancement; who keeps his ears open for every sound that can help him on his way, who keeps his hands open that he may clutch every opportunity, who is ever on the alert for everything which can help him to get on in the world, who seizes every experience in life and grinds it up into paint for his great life's picture, who keeps his heart open that he may catch every noble impulse, and everything which may inspire him—that youth will be sure to make his life successful; there are no "ifs" or "ands" about it. If he has his health, nothing can keep him from final success.

No tyranny of circumstances can permanently imprison a determined will.

The world always stands aside for the determined man.

"The general of a large army may be defeated," said Confucius, "but you cannot defeat the determined mind of a peasant."

The poor, deaf pauper, Kitto, who made shoes in the almshouse, and who became the greatest of Biblical scholars, wrote in his journal, on the threshold of manhood: "I am not myself a believer in impossibilities: I think that all the fine stories about natural ability, etc., are mere rigmarole, and that every man may, according to his opportunities and industry, render himself almost anything he wishes to become."

Lincoln is probably the most remarkable example on the pages of history, showing the possibilities of our country. From the poverty in which he was born, through the rowdyism of a frontier town, the discouragement of early bankruptcy, and the fluctuations of popular politics, he rose to the championship of union and freedom.

Lincoln's will made his way. When his friends nominated him as a candidate for the legislature, his enemies made fun of him. When making his campaign speeches he wore a mixed jean coat so short that he could not sit down on it, flax and tow-linen trousers, straw hat, and pot-metal boots. He had nothing in the world but character and friends.

When his friends suggested law to him, he laughed at the idea of his being a lawyer. He said he had not brains enough. He read law barefoot under the trees, his neighbors said, and he sometimes slept on the counter in the store where he worked. He had to borrow money to buy a suit of clothes to make a respectable appearance in the legislature, and walked to take his seat at Vandalia—100 miles.

See Thurlow Weed, defying poverty and wading through the snow two miles, with rags for shoes, to borrow a book to read before the sap-bush fire. See Locke, living on bread and water in a Dutch garret. See Heyne, sleeping many a night on a barn floor with only a book for his pillow. See Samuel Drew, tightening his apron string "in lieu of a dinner." History is full of such examples. He who will pay the price for victory need never fear final defeat.

Paris was in the hands of a mob, the authorities were panic-stricken, for they did not dare to trust their underlings. In came a man who said, "I know a young officer who has the courage and ability to quell this mob." "Send for him; send for him; send for him," said they. Napoleon was sent for, came, subjugated the mob, subjugated the authorities, ruled France, and then conquered Europe.

Success in life is dependent largely upon the willpower, and whatever weakens or impairs it diminishes success. The will can be educated. That which most easily becomes a habit in us is the will. Learn, then, to will decisively and strongly; thus fix your floating life, and leave it no longer to be carried hither and thither, like a withered leaf, by every wind that blows. "It is not talent that men lack, it is the will to labor; it is the purpose."

It was the insatiable thirst for knowledge which held to his task, through poverty and discouragement, John Leyden, a Scotch shepherd's son. Barefoot and alone, he walked six or eight miles daily to learn to read, which was all the schooling he had. His desire for an education defied the extremest poverty, and no obstacle could turn him from his purpose. He was rich when he discovered a little bookstore, and his thirsty soul would drink in the precious treasures from its priceless volumes for hours, perfectly oblivious of the scanty meal of bread and water which awaited him at his lowly lodging. Nothing could discourage him from trying to improve himself by study. It seemed to him that an opportunity to get at books and lectures was all that any man could need. Before he was 19, this poor shepherd boy with no chance had astonished the professors of Edinburgh by his knowledge of Greek and Latin.

Hearing that a surgeon's assistant in the Civil Service was wanted, although he knew nothing whatever of medicine, he determined to apply for it. There were only six months before the place was to be filled, but nothing would daunt him, and he took his degree with honor. Walter Scott, who thought this one of the most remarkable illustrations of perseverance, helped to fit him out, and he sailed for India.

Webster was very poor even after he entered Dartmouth College. A friend sent him a recipe for greasing his boots. Webster wrote and thanked him and added: "But my boots need other doctoring, for they not only admit water, but even peas and gravel stones." Yet he became one of the greatest men in the world. Sydney Smith said: "Webster was a living lie, because no man on earth could be as great as he looked." Carlyle said of him: "One would incline at sight to back him against the world."

What seemed to be luck followed Stephen Girard all his life. No matter what he did, it always seemed to others to turn to his account.

Being a foreigner, unable to speak English, short, stout, and with a repulsive face, blind in one eye, it was hard for him to get a start. But he was not the man to give up. He had begun as a cabin boy at 13, and for nine years sailed between Bordeaux and the French West Indies. He improved every leisure minute at sea, mastering the art of navigation.

At the age of eight he had first discovered that he was blind in one eye. His father, evidently thinking that he would never amount to anything, would not help him to an education beyond that of mere reading and writing, but sent his younger brothers to college. The discovery of his blindness, the neglect of his father, and the chagrin of his brothers' advancement soured his whole life.

When he began business for himself in Philadelphia, there seemed to be nothing he would not do for money. He bought and sold anything, from groceries to old junk; he bottled wine and cider, from which he made a good profit. Everything he touched prospered.

He left nothing to chance. His plans and schemes were worked out with mathematical care. His letters written to his captains in foreign ports, laying out their routes and giving detailed instructions, are models of foresight and systematic planning. He never left anything of importance to others. He was rigidly accurate in his instructions, and would not allow the slightest departure from them. He used to say that while his captains might save him money by deviating from instructions once, yet they would cause loss in 99 other cases.

He never lost a ship, and many times that which brought financial ruin to many others, as the War of 1812, only increased his wealth. Everybody, especially his jealous brother merchants, attributed his great success to his luck. While, undoubtedly, he was fortunate in happening to be at the right place at the right time, yet he was precision, method, accuracy, energy itself. What seemed luck with him was only good judgment and promptness in seizing opportunities, and the greatest care and zeal in improving them to their utmost possibilities.

The mathematician tells you that if you throw the dice, there are 30 chances to 1 against your turning up a particular number, and 100 to 1 against your repeating the same throw three times in succession: and so on in an augmenting ratio.

Many a young man who has read the story of John Wanamaker's romantic career has gained very little inspiration or help from it toward his own elevation and advancement, for he looks upon it as the result of good luck, chance, or fate. "What a lucky fellow," he says to himself as he reads; "what a bonanza he fell into!" But a careful analysis of Wanamaker's life only enforces the same lesson taught by the analysis of most great lives, namely, that a good mother, a good constitution, the habit of hard work, indomitable energy, determination which knows no defeat, decision which never wavers, a concentration which never scatters its forces, courage which never falters, self-mastery which can say No, and stick to it, strict integrity and downright honesty, a cheerful disposition, unbounded enthusiasm in one's calling, and a high aim and noble purpose ensure a very large measure of success.

Youth should be taught that there is something in circumstances;

that there is such a thing as a poor pedestrian happening to find no obstruction in his way, and reaching the goal when a better walker finds the drawbridge up, the street blockaded, and so fails to win the race; that wealth often does place unworthy sons in high positions; that family influence does gain a lawyer clients, a physician patients, an ordinary scholar a good professorship; but that, on the other hand, position, clients, patients, professorships, managers' and superintendents' positions do not necessarily constitute success. He should be taught that in the long run, as a rule, the best man does win the best place, and that persistent merit does succeed.

There is about as much chance of idleness and incapacity winning real success or a high position in life, as there would be in producing a *Paradise Lost* by shaking up promiscuously the separate words of *Webster's Dictionary* and letting them fall at random on the floor. Fortune smiles upon those who roll up their sleeves and put their shoulders to the wheel; upon men who are not afraid of dreary, dry, irksome drudgery, men of nerve and grit who do not turn aside for dirt and detail.

The youth should be taught that "he alone is great, who, by a life heroic, conquers fate"; that "diligence is the mother of good luck"; that nine times out of ten what we call luck or fate is but a mere bugbear of the indolent, the languid, the purposeless, the careless, the indifferent; that, as a rule, the man who fails does not see or seize his opportunity. Opportunity is coy, is swift, is gone, before the slow, the unobservant, the indolent, or the careless can seize her:

> *In idle wishes fools supinely stay;*
> *Be there a will and wisdom finds a way.*

It has been well said that the very reputation of being strong-willed, plucky, and indefatigable is of priceless value. It often cows enemies and dispels at the start opposition to one's undertakings which would otherwise be formidable.

It is astonishing what men who have come to their senses late in life have accomplished by a sudden resolution.

Arkwright was 50 years of age when he began to learn English grammar and improve his writing and spelling. Benjamin Franklin was past 50 before he began the study of science and philosophy. Milton, in his blindness, was past the age of 50 when he sat down to complete his world-known epic, and Scott at 55 took up his pen to redeem a liability of $600,000. "Yet I am learning," said Michael Angelo, when 70 years were past, and he had long attained the highest triumphs of his art.

Even brains are second in importance to will. The vacillating man is always pushed aside in the race of life. It is only the weak and vacillating who halt before adverse circumstances and obstacles. A man with an iron will, with a determination that nothing shall check his career, is sure, if he has perseverance and grit, to succeed. We may not find time for what we would like, but what we long for and strive for with all our strength, we usually approximate, if we do not fully reach.

I wish it were possible to show the youth of America the great part that the will might play in their success in life and in their happiness as well. The achievements of willpower are simply beyond computation. Scarcely anything in reason seems impossible to the man who can will strong enough and long enough.

How often we see this illustrated in the case of a young woman who suddenly becomes conscious that she is plain and unattractive; who, by prodigious exercise of her will and untiring industry, resolves to redeem herself from obscurity and commonness; and who not only makes up for her deficiencies, but elevates herself into a prominence and importance which mere personal attractions could never have given her! Charlotte Cushman, without a charm of form or face, climbed to the very top of her profession. How many young men, stung by consciousness of physical deformity or mental deficiencies, have, by a strong, persistent exercise of willpower, raised themselves from mediocrity and placed themselves high above those who scorned them!

History is full of examples of men and women who have redeemed themselves from disgrace, poverty, and misfortune by the firm resolution of an iron will. The consciousness of being looked upon as inferior, as incapable of accomplishing what others accomplish; the sensitiveness at being considered a dunce in school, has stung many a youth into a determination which has elevated him far above those who laughed at him, as in the case of Newton, of Adam Clark, of Sheridan, Wellington, Goldsmith, Dr. Chalmers, Curran, Disraeli, and hundreds of others.

It is men like Mirabeau, who "trample upon impossibilities"; like Napoleon, who do not wait for opportunities, but make them; like Grant, who has only "unconditional surrender" for the enemy, who change the very front of the world.

"I can't, it is impossible," said a foiled lieutenant to Alexander. "Be gone," shouted the conquering Macedonian, "there is nothing impossible to him who will try."

Were I called upon to express in a word the secret of so many failures among those who started out in life with high hopes, I should say unhesitatingly, they lacked willpower. They could not half will. What is a man without a will? He is like an engine without steam, a mere sport of chance, to be tossed about hither and thither, always at the mercy of those who have wills. I should call the strength of will the test of a young man's possibilities. Can he will strong enough, and hold whatever he undertakes with an iron grip? It is the iron grip that takes the strong hold on life. "The truest wisdom," said Napoleon, "is a resolute determination." An iron will without principle might produce a Napoleon; but with character it would make a Wellington or a Grant, untarnished by ambition or avarice.

The undivided will
Tis that compels the elements and wrings
A human music from the indifferent air.

Life is an arrow—therefore you must know What mark to aim at, how to use the bow— Then draw it to the head and let it go.

—Henry van Dyke

The important thing in life is to have a great aim, and to possess the aptitude and perseverance to attain it.

—Johann Wolfgang von Goethe

A double-minded man is unstable in all his ways.

—James 1:8

Let everyone ascertain his special business and calling, and then stick to it if he would be successful.

—Benjamin Franklin

ONE UNWAVERING AIM

"Why do you lead such a solitary life?" asked a friend of Michael Angelo. "Art is a jealous mistress," replied the artist; "she requires the whole man." During his labors at the Sistine Chapel, according to Disraeli, he refused to meet any one, even at his own house.

"This day we sailed westward, which was our course," were the simple but grand words which Columbus wrote in his journal day after day. Hope might rise and fall, terror and dismay might seize upon the crew at the mysterious variations of the compass, but Columbus, unappalled, pushed due west and nightly added to his record the above words.

"Cut an inch deeper," said a member of the Old Guard to the surgeon probing his wound, "and you will find the emperor,"—meaning his heart. By the marvelous power of concentrated purpose Napoleon had left his name on the very stones of the capital, had burned it indelibly into the heart of every Frenchman, and had left it written in living letters all over Europe. France today has not shaken off the spell of that name. In the fair city on the Seine the mystic "N" confronts you everywhere.

Oh, the power of a great purpose to work miracles! It has changed the face of the world. Napoleon knew that there were plenty of great men in France, but they did not know the might of the unwavering aim by which he was changing the destinies of Europe. He saw that what was called the "balance of power" was only an idle dream; that, unless some mastermind could be found which was a match for events, the millions would rule in anarchy. His iron will grasped the situation; and like William Pitt, he did not loiter around balancing the probabilities of failure or success or dally with his purpose.

There was no turning to the right nor to the left; no dreaming away time, nor building castles in the air; but one look and purpose, forward, upward and onward, straight to his goal. His great success in war was due largely to his definiteness of aim. He always hit the bull's-eye. He was like a great burning glass, concentrating the rays of the sun upon a single spot; he burned a hole wherever he went. After finding the weak place in the enemy's ranks, he would mass his men and hurl them like an avalanche upon the critical point, crowding volley upon volley, charge upon charge, till he made a breach. What a lesson of the power concentration there is in this man's life!

To succeed today a man must concentrate all the faculties of his mind upon one unwavering aim and have a tenacity of purpose which means death or victory. Every other inclination which tempts him from his aim must be suppressed.

A man may starve on a dozen half-learned trades or occupations; he may grow rich and famous upon one trade thoroughly mastered, even though it be the humblest.

Even Gladstone, with his ponderous yet active brain, said he could not do two things at once; he threw his entire strength upon whatever he did. The intensest energy characterized everything he undertook, even his recreation. If such concentration of energy is necessary for the success of a Gladstone, what can we common mortals hope to accomplish by "scatteration"?

All great men have been noted for their power of concentration which makes them oblivious of everything outside their aim. Victor Hugo wrote his *Notre Dame* during the revolution of 1830, while the bullets were whistling across his garden. He shut himself up in one room, locking his clothes up in another, lest they should tempt him to go out into the street, and spent most of that winter wrapped in a big gray comforter, pouring his very life into his work.

Abraham Lincoln possessed such power of concentration that he could repeat quite correctly a sermon to which he had listened in his boyhood.

A New York sportsman, in answer to an advertisement, sent 35 cents for a sure receipt to prevent a shotgun from scattering, and received the following: "Dear Sir: To keep a gun from scattering put in but a single shot."

It is the men who do one thing in this world who come to the front. Who is the favorite actor? It is a Jefferson, who devotes a lifetime to a *Rip Van Winkle*, a Booth, an Irving, a Kean, who plays one character until he can play it better than any other man living, and not the shallow players who impersonate all parts. The great man is the one who never steps outside of his specialty or dissipates his individuality. It is an Edison, a Morse, a Bell, a Howe, a Stephenson, a Watt. It is an Adam Smith, spending 10 years on the *Wealth of Nations*. It is a Gibbon, giving 20 years to his *Decline and Fall of the Roman Empire*. It is a Hume, writing 13 hours a day on his *History of England*. It is a Webster, spending 36 years on his dictionary. It is a Bancroft, working 26 years on his *History of the United States*. It is a Field, crossing the ocean 50 times to lay a cable, while the world ridicules. It is a Newton, writing his *Chronology of Ancient Kingdoms* 16 times.

A one-talent man who decides upon a definite object accomplishes more than a ten-talent man who scatters his energies and never knows exactly what he will do. The weakest living creature, by concentrating his powers upon one thing, can accomplish something; the strongest, by dispersing his over many, may fail to accomplish anything.

A great purpose is cumulative; and, like a great magnet, it attracts all that is kindred along the stream of life.

Jospeh Jefferson

413

A Yankee can splice a rope in many different ways; an English sailor only knows one way, but that is the best one. It is the one-sided man, the sharp-eyed man, the man of single and intense purpose, the man of one idea, who cuts his way through obstacles and forges to the front. The time has gone forever when a Bacon can span universal knowledge; or when, absorbing all the knowledge of the times, a Dante can sustain arguments against 14 disputants in the University of Paris, and conquer in them all. The day when a man can successfully drive a dozen callings abreast is a thing of the past. Concentration is the keynote of the century.

Scientists estimate that there is energy enough in less than 50 acres of sunshine to run all the machinery in the world, if it could be concentrated. But the sun might blaze out upon the earth forever without setting anything on fire; although these rays focused by a burning glass would melt solid granite, or even change a diamond into vapor. There are plenty of men who have ability enough; the rays of their faculties, taken separately, are all right, but they are powerless to collect them, to bring them all to bear upon a single spot. Versatile men, universal geniuses, are usually weak, because they have no power to concentrate their talents upon one point, and this makes all the difference between success and failure.

Chiseled upon the tomb of a disappointed, heartbroken king, Joseph II of Austria, in the Royal Cemetery at Vienna, a traveler tells us, is this epitaph: "Here lies a monarch who, with the best of intentions, never carried out a single plan."

Sir James Mackintosh was a man of remarkable ability. He excited in every one who knew him the greatest expectations. Many watched his career with much interest, expecting that he would dazzle the world; but there was no purpose in his life. He had intermittent attacks of enthusiasm for doing great things, but his zeal all evaporated before he could decide what to do. This fatal defect in his character kept him balancing between conflicting motives; and his whole life was almost thrown away. He lacked power to choose one object and persevere with a single aim, sacrificing every interfering inclination. He, for instance, vacillated for weeks trying to determine whether to use "usefulness" or "utility" in a composition.

One talent utilized in a single direction will do infinitely more than 10 talents scattered. A thimbleful of powder behind a ball in a rifle will do more execution than a carload of powder unconfined. The rifle barrel is the purpose that gives direct aim to the powder, which otherwise, no matter how good it might be, would be powerless. The poorest scholar in school or college often, in practical life, far outstrips the class leader or senior wrangler, simply because what little ability he has he employs for a definite object, while the other, depending upon his general ability and brilliant prospects, never concentrates his powers.

It is fashionable to ridicule the man of one idea, but the men who have changed the front of the world have been men of a single aim. No man can make his mark on this age of specialties who is not a man of one idea, one supreme air, one master passion. The man who would make himself felt on this bustling planet, who would make a breach in the compact conservatism of our civilization, must play all his guns on one point. A wavering aim, a faltering purpose, has no place in the twentieth century. "Mental shiftlessness" is the cause of many a failure. The world is full of unsuccessful men who spend their lives letting empty buckets down into empty wells.

"Mr. A. often laughs at me," said a young American chemist, "because I have but one idea. He talks about everything, aims to excel in many things; but I have learned that, if I ever wish to make a breach, I must play my guns continually upon one point." This great chemist, when an obscure schoolmaster, used to study by the light of a pine knot in a log cabin. Not many years later he was performing experiments in electromagnetism before English earls, and subsequently he was at the head of one of the largest scientific institutes of this country. He was the late Professor Henry, of the Smithsonian Institution, Washington.

We should guard against a talent which we cannot hope to practice in perfection, says Goethe. Improve it as we may, we shall always, in the end, when the merit of the matter has become apparent to us, painfully lament the loss of time and strength devoted to such botching. An old proverb says: "The master of one trade will support a wife and seven children, and the master of seven will not support himself."

It is the single aim that wins. Men with monopolizing ambitions rarely live in history. They do not focus their powers long enough to burn their names indelibly into the honor roll. Edward Everett, even with his magnificent powers, disappointed the expectations of his friends. He spread himself over the whole field of knowledge and elegant culture; but the mention of the name of Everett does not call up any one great achievement as does that of names like Garrison and

Phillips. Voltaire called the Frenchman La Harpe an oven which was always heating, but which never cooked anything. Hartley Coleridge was splendidly endowed with talent, but there was one fatal lack in his character—he had no definite purpose, and his life was a failure. Unstable as water, he could not excel.

Southey, the uncle of Coleridge, said of him: "Coleridge has two left hands." He was so morbidly shy from living alone in his dreamland that he could not open a letter without trembling. He would often rally from his purposeless life, and resolve to redeem himself from the oblivion he saw staring him in the face; but, like Sir James Mackintosh, he remained a man of promise merely to the end of his life.

The man who succeeds has a program. He fires his course and adheres to it. He lays his plans and executes them. He goes straight to his goal. He is not pushed this way and that every time a difficulty is thrown in his path; if he cannot get over it, he goes through it. Constant and steady use of the faculties under a central purpose gives strength and power, while the use of faculties without an aim or end only weakens them. The mind must be focused on a definite end, or, like machinery without a balance wheel, it will rack itself to pieces.

This age of concentration calls, not for educated men merely, not for talented men, not for geniuses, not for jacks-of-all-trades, but for men who are trained to do one thing as well as it can be done. Napoleon could go through the drill of his soldiers better than any one of his men.

Stick to your aim. The constant changing of one's occupation is fatal to all success. After a young man has spent five or six years in a dry goods store, he concludes that he would rather sell groceries, thereby throwing away five years of valuable experience which will be of very little use to him in the grocery business; and so he spends a large part of his life drifting around from one kind of employment to another, learning part of each but all of none, forgetting that experience is worth more to him than money and that the years devoted to learning his trade or occupation are the most valuable. Half-learned trades, no matter if a man has twenty, will never give him a good living, much less a competency, while wealth is absolutely out of the question.

How many young men fail to reach the point of efficiency in one line of work before they get discouraged and venture into something else! How easy to see the thorns in one's own profession or vocation, and only the roses in that of another! A young man in business, for instance, seeing a physician riding about town in his carriage, visiting his patients, imagines that a doctor must have an easy, ideal life, and wonders that he himself should have embarked in an occupation so full of disagreeable drudgery and hardships. He does not know of the years of dry, tedious study which the physician has consumed, the months and perhaps years of waiting for patients, the dry detail of anatomy, the endless names of drugs and technical terms.

There is a sense of great power in a vocation after a man has reached the point of efficiency in it, the point of productiveness, the point where his skill begins to tell and brings in returns. Up to this point of efficiency, while he is learning his trade, the time seems to have been almost thrown away. But he has been storing up a vast reserve of knowledge of detail, laying foundations, forming his acquaintances, gaining his reputation for truthfulness, trustworthiness, and integrity, and in establishing his credit. When he reaches this point of efficiency, all the knowledge and skill, character, influence, and credit thus gained come to his aid, and he soon finds that in what seemed almost thrown away lies the secret of his prosperity. The credit he established as a clerk, the confidence, the integrity, the friendships formed, he finds equal to a large capital when he starts out for himself and takes the highway to fortune; while the young man who half learned several trades, got discouraged and stopped just short of the point of efficiency, just this side of success, is a failure because he didn't go far enough; he did not press on to the point at which his acquisition would have been profitable.

In spite of the fact that nearly all very successful men have made a lifework of one thing, we see on every hand hundreds of young men and women flitting about from occupation to occupation, trade to trade, in one thing today and another tomorrow—just as though they could go from one thing to another by turning a switch, as though they could run as well on another track as on the one they have left, regardless of the fact that no two careers have the same gage, that every man builds his own road upon which another man's engine cannot run either with speed or safety. This fickleness, this disposition to shift about from one occupation to another, seems to be peculiar to American life, so much so that, when a young man meets a friend whom he has not seen for some time, the commonest question to ask is, "What are you doing now?" showing the improbability or uncertainty that he is doing today what he was doing when they last met.

Some people think that if they "keep everlastingly at it" they will succeed, but this is not always so. Working without a plan is as foolish as going to sea without a compass.

A ship which has broken its rudder in mid-ocean may "keep everlastingly at it," may keep on a full head of steam, driving about all the time, but it never arrives anywhere, it never reaches any port unless by accident; and if it does find a haven, its cargo may not be suited to the people, the climate, or conditions. The ship must be directed to a definite port, for which its cargo is adapted, and where there is a demand for it, and it must aim steadily for that port through sunshine and storm, through tempest and fog.

So, a man who would succeed must not drift about rudderless on the ocean of life. He must not only steer straight toward his destined port when the ocean is smooth, when the currents and winds serve, but he must keep his course in the very teeth of the wind and the tempest, and even when enveloped in the fogs of disappointment and mists of opposition. Atlantic liners do not stop for fogs or storms; they plow straight through the rough seas with only one thing in view, their destined port, and no matter what the weather is, no matter what obstacles they encounter, their arrival in port can be predicted to within a few hours.

On the prairies of South America there grows a flower that always inclines in the same direction. If a traveler loses his way and has neither compass nor chart, by turning to this flower he will find a guide on which he can implicitly rely; for no matter how the rains descend or the winds blow, its leaves point to the north. So, there are many men whose purposes are so well known, whose aims are so constant, that no matter what difficulties they may encounter, or what opposition they may meet, you can tell almost to a certainty where they will come out. They may be delayed by head winds and counter currents, but they will always head for the port and will steer straight towards the harbor. You know to a certainty that whatever else they may lose, they will not lose their compass or rudder.

Whatever may happen to a man of this stamp, even though his sails may be swept away and his mast stripped to the deck, though he may be wrecked by the storms of life, the needle of his compass will still point to the North Star of his hope. Whatever comes, his life will not be purposeless. Even a wreck that makes its port is a greater success than a full-rigged ship with all its sails flying, with every mast and every rope intact, which merely drifts along into an accidental harbor.

To fix a wandering life and give it direction is not an easy task, but a life which has no definite aim is sure to be frittered away in empty and purposeless dreams. "Listless triflers," "busy idlers," "purposeless busybodies," are seen everywhere. A healthy, definite purpose is a remedy for a thousand ills which attend aimless lives. Discontent and dissatisfaction flee before a definite purpose. What we do begrudgingly without a purpose becomes a delight with one, and no work is well done nor healthily done which is not enthusiastically done.

Mere energy is not enough; it must be concentrated on some steady, unwavering aim. What is more common than "unsuccessful geniuses," or failures with "commanding talents"? Indeed, the term "unrewarded genius" has become a proverb. Every town has unsuccessful educated and talented men. But education is of no value, talent is worthless, unless it can do something, achieve something. Men who can do something at everything and a very little at anything are not wanted in this age.

What this age wants is young men and women who can do one thing without losing their identity or individuality, or becoming narrow, cramped, or dwarfed. Nothing can take the place of an all-absorbing purpose; education cannot, genius cannot, talent cannot, industry cannot, willpower cannot. The purposeless life must ever be a failure. What good are powers, faculties, unless we can use them for a purpose? What good would a chest of tools do a carpenter unless he could use them? A college education, a head full of knowledge, are worth little to the men who cannot use them to some definite end.

The man without a purpose never leaves his mark upon the world. He has no individuality; he is absorbed in the mass, lost in the crowd, weak, wavering, and incompetent.

"Consider, my lord," said Rowland Hill to the Prime Minister of England, "that a letter to Ireland and the answer back would cost thousands upon thousands of my affectionate countrymen more than a fifth of their week's wages. If you shut the post office to them, which you do now, you shut out warm hearts and generous affections from home, kindred, and friends." The lad learned that it cost to carry a letter from London to Edinburgh, 404 miles, one eighteenth of a cent, while the government charged for a simple folded sheet of paper 28 cents, and twice as much if there was the smallest enclosure. Against the opposition and contempt of the post office department he at length carried his point, and on January 10, 1840, penny postage was established throughout Great Britain. Mr. Hill was chosen to introduce the system, at a salary of 1,500 pounds a year. His success was most encouraging, but at the end of two years a Tory minister dismissed him without paying for his services, as agreed.

The public was indignant, and at once contributed 65,000 dollars; and, at the request of Queen Victoria, Parliament voted him 100,000 dollars cash, together with 10,000 dollars a year for life.

It is a great purpose which gives meaning to life; it unifies all our powers, binds them together in one cable and makes strong and united what was weak, separated, scattered.

"Smatterers" are weak and superficial. Of what use is a man who knows a little of everything and not much of anything? It is the momentum of constantly repeated acts that tells the story. "Let thine eyes look straight before thee. Ponder the path of thy feet and let all thy ways be established. Turn not to the right hand nor to the left." One great secret of St. Paul's power lay in his strong purpose. Nothing could daunt, nothing intimidate him. The Roman Emperor could not muzzle him, the dungeon could not appall him, no prison suppress him, obstacles could not discourage him. "This one thing I do" was written all over his work. The quenchless zeal of his mighty purpose burned its way down through the centuries, and its contagion will never cease to fire the hearts of men.

"Try and come home somebody," said his mother to Gambetta as she sent him off to Paris to school. Poverty pinched this lad hard in his little garret study and his clothes were shabby, but what of that? He had made up his mind to get on in the world. For years he was chained to his desk and worked like a hero. At last, his opportunity came. Jules Favre was to plead a great cause on a certain day; but, being ill, he chose this young man, absolutely unknown, rough and uncouth, to take his place.

For many years Gambetta had been preparing for such an opportunity, and he was equal to it. He made one of the greatest speeches that up to that time had ever been made in France. That night all the papers in Paris were sounding the praises of this ragged, uncouth Bohemian, and soon all France recognized him as the Republican leader. This sudden rise was not due to luck or accident. He had been steadfastly working and fighting his way up against oppositions and poverty for just such an occasion. Had he not been equal to it, it would only have made him ridiculous. What a stride; yesterday, poor and unknown, living in a garret; today, deputy-elect, in the city of Marseilles, and the great Republican leader!

When Louis Napoleon had been defeated at Sedan and had delivered his sword to William of Prussia, and when the Prussian army was marching on Paris, the brave Gambetta went out of the besieged city in a balloon barely grazed by the Prussian guns, landed in Amiens, and by almost superhuman skill raised three armies of 800,000 men, provided for their maintenance, and directed their military operations. A German officer said: "This colossal energy is the most remarkable event of modern history, and will carry down Gambetta's name to remote posterity." This youth who was poring over his books in an attic while other youths were promenading the Champs-Élysées, although but 32 years old, was now virtually dictator of France, and the greatest orator in the Republic.

What a striking example of the great reserve of personal power, which, even in dissolute lives, is sometimes called out by a great emergency or sudden sorrow, and ever after leads the life to victory! When Gambetta found that his first speech had electrified all France, his great reserve rushed to the front; he was suddenly weaned from dissipation, and resolved to make his mark in the world. Nor did he lose his head in his quick leap into fame. He still lived in the upper room in the musty Latin Quarter, and remained a poor man, without stain of dishonor, though he might easily have made himself a millionaire. When he died the *Figaro* said, "The Republic has lost its greatest man." American boys should study this great man, for he loved our country, and took our Republic as the pattern for France.

There is no grander sight in the world than that of a young man fired with a great purpose, dominated by one unwavering aim. He is bound to win; the world stands to one side and lets him pass; it always makes way for the man with a will in him. He does not have one half the opposition to overcome that the undecided, purposeless man has who, like driftwood, runs against all sorts of snags to which he must yield simply because he has no momentum to force them out of his way. What a sublime spectacle it is to see a youth going straight to his goal, cutting his way through difficulties, and surmounting obstacles which dishearten others, as though they were but stepping stones! Defeat, like a gymnasium, only gives him new power; opposition only doubles his exertions; dangers only increase his courage. No matter what comes to him, sickness, poverty, disaster, he never turns his eye from his goal.

Duos qui sequitur lepores, neutrum capit.

What we do upon some great occasion will probably depend on what we already are; and what we are will be the result of previous years of self-discipline.

—H.P. Liddon

I consider a human soul without education like marble in a quarry, which shows none of its inherent beauties until the skill of the polisher sketches out the colors, makes the surface shine, and discovers every ornamental cloud, spot, and vein that runs throughout the body of it.

—Joseph Addison

Use your gifts faithfully, and they shall be enlarged; practice what you know, and you shall attain to higher knowledge.

—Matthew Arnold

Haste trips up its own heels, fetters and stops itself.

—Seneca

The more you know, the more you can save yourself and that which belongs to you, and do more work with less effort.

—Charles Kingsley

WORK AND WAIT

"I was a mere cipher in that vast sea of human enterprise," said Henry Bessemer, speaking of his arrival in London in 1831. Although but 18 years old, and without an acquaintance in the city, he soon made work for himself by inventing a process of copying bas-reliefs on cardboard. His method was so simple that one could learn in 10 minutes how to make a die from an embossed stamp for a penny. Having ascertained later that in this way the raised stamps on all official papers in England could easily be forged, he set to work and invented a perforated stamp which could not be forged nor removed from a document. At the public stamp office, he was told by the chief that the government was losing 100,000 pounds a year through the custom of removing stamps from old parchments and using them again.

The chief also fully appreciated the new danger of easy counterfeiting. So, he offered Bessemer a definite sum for his process of perforation, or an office for life at 800 pounds a year. Bessemer chose the office, and hastened to tell the good news to a young woman with whom he had agreed to share his fortune. In explaining his invention, he told how it would prevent anyone from taking a valuable stamp from a document a hundred years old and using it a second time.

"Yes," said his betrothed, "I understand that; but surely, if all stamps had a date put upon them, they could not at a future time be used without detection."

This was a very short speech, and of no special importance if we omit a single word of four letters; but, like the schoolboy's pins which saved the lives of thousands of people annually by not getting swallowed, that little word, by keeping out of the ponderous minds of the British revenue officers, had for a long period saved the government the burden of caring for an additional income of 100,000 pounds a year. And the same little word, if published in its connection, would render Bessemer's perforation device of far less value than a last year's bird's nest. He felt proud of the young woman's ingenuity, and promptly suggested the improvement at the stamp office.

As a result, his system of perforation was abandoned and he was deprived of his promised office, the government coolly making use from that day to this, without compensation, of the idea conveyed by that little insignificant word.

So, Bessemer's financial prospects were not very encouraging; but, realizing that the best capital a young man can have is a capital wife, he at once entered into a partnership which placed at his command the combined ideas of two very level heads. The result, after years of thought and experiment, was the Bessemer process of making steel cheaply, which has revolutionized the iron industry throughout the world. His method consists simply in forcing hot air from below into several tons of melted pig iron, so as to produce intense combustion; and then adding enough spiegeleisen (specular iron), an ore rich in carbon, to change the whole mass to steel.

He discovered this simple process only after trying in vain much more difficult and expensive methods.

All things come round to him who will but wait.

The great lack of the age is want of thoroughness. How seldom you find a young man or woman who is willing to take time to prepare for his life work! A little education is all they want, a little smattering of books, and then they are ready for business.

"Can't wait" is characteristic of the century, and is written on everything; on commerce, on schools, on society, on churches. Can't wait for a high school, seminary, or college. The boy can't wait to become a youth, nor the youth a man. Youth rush into business with no great reserve of education or drill; of course they do poor, feverish work, and break down in middle life, and many die of old age in the forties. Everybody is in a hurry. Buildings are rushed up so quickly that they will not stand, and everything is made "to sell."

Not long ago a professor in one of our universities had a letter from a young woman in the West, asking him if he did not think she could teach elocution if she could come to the university and take 12 lessons. Our young people of today are not willing to lay broad, deep foundations. The weary years in preparatory school and college dishearten them. They only want a "smattering" of an education. But as Pope says,

> *A little learning is a dangerous thing;*
> *Drink deep, or taste not the Pierian spring:*
> *There shallow draughts intoxicate the brain,*
> *And drinking largely sobers us again.*

The shifts to cover up ignorance, and "the constant trembling lest some blunder should expose one's emptiness," are pitiable. Short cuts and abridged methods are the demand of the hour. But the way to shorten the road to success is to take plenty of time to lay in your reserve power. Hard work, a definite aim, and faithfulness will shorten the way. Don't risk a life's superstructure upon a day's foundation.

Patience is Nature's motto. She works ages to bring a flower to perfection. What will she not do for the greatest of her creation? Ages and eons are nothing to her; out of them she has been carving her great statue, a perfect man.

Johnson said a man must turn over half a library to write one book. When an authoress told Wordsworth she had spent six hours on a poem, he replied that he would have spent six weeks. Think of Bishop Hall spending 30 years on one of his works! Owens was working on the *Commentary to the Epistle to the Hebrews* for 20 years. Moore spent several weeks on one of his musical stanzas which reads as if it were a dash of genius.

Carlyle wrote with the utmost difficulty and never executed a page of his great histories till he had consulted every known authority, so that every sentence is the quintessence of many books, the product of many hours of drudging research in the great libraries. Today, *Sartor Resartus* is everywhere. You can get it for a mere trifle at almost any bookseller's, and hundreds of thousands of copies are scattered over the world. But when Carlyle brought it to London in 1851, it was refused almost contemptuously by three prominent publishers. At length he managed to get it into *Fraser's Magazine*, the editor of which conveyed to the author the pleasing information that his work had been received with "unqualified disapprobation."

Henry Ward Beecher sent half a dozen articles to the publisher of a religious paper to pay for his subscription, but they were respectfully declined. The publishers of the *Atlantic Monthly* returned Miss Alcott's manuscript, suggesting that she had better stick to teaching. One of the leading magazines ridiculed Tennyson's first poems, and consigned the young poet to temporary oblivion. Only one of Ralph Waldo Emerson's books had a remunerative sale. Washington Irving was nearly 70 years old before the income from his books paid the expenses of his household.

In some respects, it is very unfortunate that the old system of binding boys out to a trade has been abandoned. Today very few boys learn any trade. They pick up what they know, as they go along, just as a student crams for a particular examination, just to "get through," without any effort to see how much he may learn on any subject.

Think of an American youth spending 10 years with da Vinci on the model of an equestrian statue that he might master the anatomy of the horse! Most young American artists would expect, in a quarter of that time, to sculpture an *Apollo Belvidere*.

A rich man asked Howard Burnett to do a little something for his album. Burnett complied and charged 1,000 francs. "But it took you only five minutes," objected the rich man. "Yes, but it took me 30 years to learn how to do it in five minutes."

What the age wants is men who have the nerve and the grit to work and wait, whether the world applaud or hiss; a Mirabeau, who can struggle on for 40 years before he has a chance to show the world his vast reserve, destined to shake an empire; a Farragut, a Von Moltke, who have the persistence to work and wait for half a century for their first great opportunities; a Grant, fighting on in heroic silence, when denounced by his brother generals and politicians everywhere; a Michael Angelo, working seven long years decorating the Sistine Chapel with his matchless *Creation* and the *Last Judgment*, refusing all remuneration therefor, lest his pencil might catch the taint of avarice; a Thurlow Weed, walking two miles through the snow with rags tied around his feet for shoes, to borrow *A History of the French Revolution*, and eagerly devouring it before the sap-bush fire; a Milton, elaborating *Paradise Lost* in a world he could not see; a Thackeray, struggling on cheerfully after his *Vanity Fair* was refused by a dozen publishers; a Balzac, toiling and waiting in a lonely garret; men whom neither poverty, debt, nor hunger could discourage or intimidate; not daunted by privations, not hindered by discouragements. It wants men who can work and wait.

When a young lawyer Daniel Webster once looked in vain through all the law libraries near him, and then ordered at an expense of 50 dollars the necessary books, to obtain authorities and precedents in a case in which his client was a poor blacksmith. He won his case, but, on account of the poverty of his client, only charged 15 dollars, thus losing heavily on the books bought, to say nothing of his time. Years after, as he was passing through New York City, he was consulted by Aaron Burr on an important but puzzling case then pending before the Supreme Court. He saw in a moment that it was just like the blacksmith's case, an intricate question of title, which he had solved so thoroughly that it was to him now as simple as the multiplication table.

Going back to the time of Charles II he gave the law and precedents involved with such readiness and accuracy of sequence that Burr asked in great surprise if he had been consulted before in the case. "Most certainly not," he replied, "I never heard of your case till this evening." "Very well," said Burr, "proceed"; and, when he had finished, Webster received a fee that paid him liberally for all the time and trouble he had spent for his early client.

Albert Bierstadt first crossed the Rocky Mountains with a band of pioneers in 1859, making sketches for the paintings of Western scenes for which he had become famous. As he followed the trail to Pike's Peak, he gazed in wonder upon the enormous herds of buffaloes which dotted the plains as far as the eye could reach, and thought of the time when they would have disappeared before the march of civilization. The thought haunted him and found its final embodiment in *The Last of the Buffaloes* in 1890. To perfect this great work he had spent 20 years.

Everything which endures, which will stand the test of time, must have a deep, solid foundation. In Rome the foundation is often the most expensive part of an edifice, so deep must they dig to build on the living rock.

Fifty feet of the Bunker Hill Monument are under ground; unseen and unappreciated by those who tread about that historic shaft, but it is this foundation, apparently thrown away, which enables it to stand upright, true to the plumbline through all the tempests that lash its granite sides. A large part of every successful life must be spent in laying foundation stones underground. Success is the child of drudgery and perseverance and depends upon "knowing how long it takes to succeed."

Endurance is a much better test of character than any one act of heroism, however noble.

The pianist Thalberg said he never ventured to perform one of his celebrated pieces in public until he had played it at least 1,500 times. He laid no claim whatever to genius; he said it was all a question of hard work. The accomplishments of such industry, such perseverance, would put to shame many a man who claims genius.

Before Edmund Kean would consent to appear in that character which he acted with such consummate skill, the *Gentleman Villain*, he practiced constantly before a glass, studying expression for a year and a half. When he appeared upon the stage, Byron, who went with Moore to see him, said he never looked upon so fearful and wicked a face. As the great actor went on to delineate the terrible consequences of sin, Byron fainted.

"For years I was in my place of business by sunrise," said a wealthy banker who had begun without a dollar; "and often I did not leave it for 15 or 18 hours."

Patience, it is said, changes the mulberry leaf to satin. The giant oak on the hillside was detained months or years in its upward growth while its root took a great turn around some rock, in order to gain a hold by which the tree was anchored to withstand the storms of centuries. Da Vinci spent four years on the head of *Mona Lisa*, perhaps the most beautiful ever painted, but he left therein an artistic thought for all time.

Said Captain Bingham: "You can have no idea of the wonderful machine that the German army is and how well it is prepared for war. A chart is made out which shows just what must be done in the case of wars with the different nations, and every officer's place in the scheme is laid out beforehand. There is a schedule of trains which will supersede all other schedules the moment war is declared, and this is so arranged that the commander of the army here could telegraph to any officer to take such a train and go to such a place at a moment's notice."

A learned clergyman was thus accosted by an illiterate preacher who despised education: "Sir, you have been to college, I presume?" "Yes, sir," was the reply. "I am thankful," said the former, "that the Lord opened my mouth without any learning." "A similar event," retorted the clergyman, "happened in Balaam's time."

A young man just graduated told the President of Trinity College that he had completed his education and had come to say goodbye. "Indeed," said the President, "I have just begun my education."

Many an extraordinary man has been made out of a very ordinary boy: but in order to accomplish this we must begin with him while he is young. It is simply astonishing what training will do for a rough, uncouth, and even dull lad, if he has good material in him, and comes under the tutelage of a skilled educator before his habits become fixed or confirmed.

Even a few weeks' or months' drill of the rawest and roughest recruits in the late Civil War so straightened and dignified stooping and uncouth soldiers, and made them manly, erect, and courteous in their bearing, that their own friends scarcely knew them. If this change is so marked in the youth who has grown to maturity, what a miracle is possible in the lad who is taken early and put under a course of drill and systematic training, both physical, mental, and moral! How often a man who is in the penitentiary, in the poorhouse, or among the tramps, or living out a miserable existence in the slums of our cities, rough, slovenly, has slumbering within the rags possibilities which would have developed him into a magnificent man, an ornament to the human race instead of a foul blot and ugly scar, had he only been fortunate enough early in life to have enjoyed the benefits of efficient and systematic training!

Laziness begins in cobwebs and ends in iron chains. Edison described his repeated efforts to make the phonograph reproduce an aspirated sound and added: "From 18 to 20 hours a day for the last 7 months I have worked on this single word 'specia.' I said into the phonograph 'specia, specia, specia,' but the instrument responded 'pecia, pecia, pecia.' It was enough to drive one mad. But I held firm, and I have succeeded."

The road to distinction must be paved with years of self-denial and hard work.

Horace Mann, the great author of the common school system of Massachusetts, was a remarkable example of that pluck and patience which can work and wait. His only inheritance was poverty and hard work. But he had an unquenchable thirst for knowledge and a determination to get on in the world. He braided straw to earn money to buy books for which his soul thirsted.

Gladstone was bound to win. Although he had spent many years of preparation for his life work, in spite of the consciousness of marvelous natural endowments which would have been deemed sufficient by many young men, and notwithstanding he had gained the coveted prize of a seat in Parliament, yet he decided to make himself master of the situation; and amid all his public and private duties, he not only spent 11 terms more in the study of the law, but also studied Greek constantly and read every well-written book or paper he could obtain, so determined was he that his life should be rounded out to its fullest measure, and that his mind should have broad and liberal culture.

Ole Bull said: "If I practice one day, I can see the result; if I practice two days, my friends can see it; if I practice three days, the great public can see it."

The habit of seizing every bit of knowledge, no matter how insignificant it may seem at the time, every opportunity, every occasion, and grinding them all up into experience, cannot be overestimated. You will find use for all of it. Webster once repeated with effect an anecdote which he had heard 14 years before, and which he had not thought of in the meantime. It exactly fitted the occasion. "It is an ill mason that rejects any stone."

Webster was once urged to speak on a subject of great importance, but refused, saying he was very busy and had no time to master the subject. "But," replied his friend, "a very few words from you would do much to awaken public attention to it." Webster replied, "If there be so much weight in my words, it is because I do not allow myself to speak on any subject until my mind is imbued with it." On one occasion Webster made a remarkable speech before the Phi Beta Kappa Society at Harvard, when a book was presented to him; but after he had gone, his "impromptu" speech, carefully written out, was found in the book which he had forgotten to take away.

Demosthenes was once asked to speak on a great and sudden emergency, but replied, "I am not prepared." In fact, it was thought by many that Demosthenes did not possess any genius whatever, because he never allowed himself to speak on any subject without thorough preparation. In any meeting or assembly, when called upon, he would never rise, even to make remarks, it was said, without previously preparing himself.

Alexander Hamilton said, "Men give me credit for genius. All the genius I have lies just in this: when I have a subject in hand, I study it profoundly. Day and night it is before me. I explore it in all its bearings. My mind becomes pervaded with it. Then the effort which I make the people are pleased to call the fruit of genius; it is the fruit of labor and thought." The law of labor is equally binding on genius and mediocrity.

Nelaton, the great surgeon, said that if he had four minutes in which to perform an operation on which a life depended, he would take one minute to consider how best to do it.

"Many men," says Longfellow, "do not allow their principles to take root, but pull them up every now and then, as children do flowers they have planted, to see if they are growing." We must not only work, but also wait.

"The spruce young spark," says Sizer, "who thinks chiefly of his mustache and boots and shiny hat, of getting along nicely and easily during the day, and talking about the theater, the opera, or a fast horse, ridiculing the faithful young fellow who came to learn the business and make a man of himself because he will not join in wasting his time in dissipation, will see the day, if his useless life is not earlier blasted by vicious indulgences, when he will be glad to accept a situation from the fellow clerk whom he now ridicules and affects to despise, when the latter shall stand in the firm, dispensing benefits and acquiring fortune."

"I have been watching the careers of young men by the thousand in this busy city of New York for over 30 years," said Dr. Cuyler, "and I find that the chief difference between the successful and the failures lies in the single element of staying power. Permanent success is oftener won by holding on than by sudden dash, however brilliant. The easily discouraged, who are pushed back by a straw, are all the time dropping to the rear—to perish or to be carried along on the stretcher of charity. They who understand and practice Abraham Lincoln's homely maxim of 'pegging away' have achieved the solidest success."

The Duke of Wellington became so discouraged because he did not advance in the army that he applied for a much inferior position in the customs department, but was refused. Napoleon had applied for every vacant position for seven years before he was recognized, but meanwhile he studied with all his might, supplementing what was considered a thorough military education by researches and reflections which in later years enabled him easily to teach the art of war to veterans who had never dreamed of his novel combinations.

Reserves which carry us through great emergencies are the result of long working and long waiting. Dr. Collyer declares that reserves mean to a man also achievement: "The power to do the grandest thing possible to your nature when you feel you must, or some precious thing will be lost—to do well always, but best in the crisis on which all things turn; to stand the strain of a long fight, and still find you have something left, and so to never know you are beaten, because you never are beaten."

He only is independent in action who has been earnest and thorough in preparation and self-culture. "Not for school, but for life, we learn"; and our habits—of promptness, earnestness, and thoroughness, or of tardiness, fickleness, and superficiality—are the things acquired most readily and longest retained.

To vary the language of another, the three great essentials to success in mental and physical labor are Practice, Patience, and Perseverance, but the greatest of these is Perseverance.

> *Let us, then, be up and doing,*
> *With a heart for any fate;*
> *Still achieving, still pursuing,*
> *Learn to labor and to wait.*

Think naught a trifle, though it small appear; Small sands the mountain, moments make the year, And trifles, life.

—Edward Young

It is but the littleness of man that sees no greatness in trifles.

—Wendell Phillips

He that despiseth small things shall fall by little and little.

—Ecclesiasticus 19:1

The creation of a thousand forests is in one acorn.

—Ralph Waldo Emerson

Men are led by trifles.

—Napoleon

A pebble on the streamlet scant
Has turned the course of many a river.
The bad thing about a little sin is that it won't stay little.

THE MIGHT OF LITTLE THINGS

"Arletta's pretty feet, glistening in the brook, made her the mother of William the Conqueror," says Palgrave's *History of Normandy and England*. "Had she not thus fascinated Duke Robert the Liberal, of Normandy, Harold would not have fallen at Hastings, no Anglo-Norman dynasty could have arisen, no British Empire."

We may tell which way the wind blew before the Deluge by marking the ripple and cupping of the rain in the petrified sand now preserved forever. We tell the very path by which gigantic creatures, whom man never saw, walked to the river's edge to find their food.

It was little Greece that rolled back the overflowing tide of Asiatic luxury and despotism, giving instead to Europe and America models of the highest political freedom yet attained, and germs of limitless mental growth. A different result at Plataea would have delayed the progress of humanity more than 10 centuries.

Among the lofty Alps, it is said, the guides sometimes demand absolute silence, lest the vibration of the voice bring down an avalanche.

The power of observation in the American Indian would put many an educated man to shame. Returning home, an Indian discovered that his venison, which had been hanging up to dry, had been stolen. After careful observation he started to track the thief through the woods. Meeting a man on the route, he asked him if he had seen a little, old, white man, with a short gun, and with a small bobtailed dog. The man told him he had met such a man, but was surprised to find that the Indian had not even seen the one he described, and asked him how he could give such a minute description of the man he had never seen. "I knew the thief was a little man," said the Indian, "because he rolled up a stone to stand on in order to reach the venison; I knew he was an old man by his short steps; I knew he was a white man by his turning out his toes in walking, which an Indian never does; I knew he had a short gun by the mark it left on the tree where he had stood it up; I knew the dog was small by his tracks and short steps, and that he had a bobtail by the mark it left in the dust where he sat."

Two drops of rain, falling side by side, were separated a few inches by a gentle breeze. Striking on opposite sides of the roof of a courthouse in Wisconsin, one rolled southward through the Rock River and the Mississippi to the Gulf of Mexico; while the other entered successively the Fox River, Green Bay, Lake Michigan, the Straits of Mackinaw, Lake Huron, St. Clair River, Lake St. Clair, Detroit River, Lake Erie, Niagara River, Lake Ontario, the St. Lawrence River, and finally reached the Gulf of St. Lawrence. How slight the influence of the breeze, yet such was the formation of the continent that a trifling cause was multiplied almost beyond the power of figures to express its momentous effect upon the destinies of these companion raindrops. Who can calculate the future of the smallest trifle when a mud crack swells to an Amazon and the stealing of a penny may end on the scaffold? The act of a moment may cause a life's regret. A trigger may be pulled in an instant, but the soul returns never.

A spark falling upon some combustibles led to the invention of gunpowder. A few bits of seaweed and driftwood, floating on the waves, enabled Columbus to stay a mutiny of his sailors which threatened to prevent the discovery of a new world. There are moments in history which balance years of ordinary life. Dana could interest a class for hours on a grain of sand; and from a single bone, such as no one had ever seen before, Agassiz could deduce the entire structure and habits of an animal which no man had ever seen so accurately that subsequent discoveries of complete skeletons have not changed one of his conclusions.

A cricket once saved a military expedition from destruction. The commanding officer and hundreds of his men were going to South America on a great ship, and, through the carelessness of the watch, they would have been dashed upon a ledge of rock had it not been for a cricket which a soldier had brought on board. When the little insect scented the land, it broke its long silence by a shrill note, and thus warned them of their danger.

By gnawing through a dike, even a rat may drown a nation. A little boy in Holland saw water trickling from a small hole near the bottom of a dike. He realized that the leak would rapidly become larger if the water were not checked, so he held his hand over the hole for hours on a dark and dismal night until he could attract the attention of passersby. His name is still held in grateful remembrance in Holland.

The beetling chalk cliffs of England were built by rhizopods, too small to be clearly seen without the aid of a magnifying glass.

What was so unlikely as that throwing an empty wine flask in the fire should furnish the first notion of a locomotive, or that the sickness of an Italian chemist's wife and her absurd craving for reptiles for food should begin the electric telegraph. Madame Galvani noticed the contraction of the muscles of a skinned frog which was accidentally touched at the moment her husband took a spark from an electrical machine. She gave the hint which led to the discovery of galvanic electricity, now so useful in the arts and in transmitting vocal or written language.

"The fate of a nation," says Gladstone, "has often depended upon the good or bad digestion of a fine dinner."

A stamp act to raise 60,000 pounds produced the American Revolution, a war that cost England 100,000,000 pounds. A war between France and England, costing more than 100,000 lives, grew out of a quarrel as to which of two vessels should first be served with water. The quarrel of two Indian boys over a grasshopper led to the "Grasshopper War." What mighty contests rise from trivial things!

A young man once went to India to seek his fortune, but, finding no opening, he went to his room, loaded his pistol, put the muzzle to his head, and pulled the trigger. But it did not go off. He went to the window to point it in another direction and try it again, resolved that if the weapon went off, he would regard it as a Providence that he was spared. He pulled the trigger and it went off the first time. Trembling with excitement he resolved to hold his life sacred, to make the most of it, and never again to cheapen it. This young man became General Robert Clive, who, with but a handful of European soldiers, secured to the East India Company and afterwards to Great Britain a great and rich country with two hundred millions of people.

The cackling of a goose aroused the sentinels and saved Rome from the Gauls, and the pain from a thistle warned a Scottish army of the approach of the Danes.

Henry Ward Beecher came within one vote of being elected superintendent of a railway. If he had had that vote America would probably have lost its greatest preacher. What a little thing fixes destiny!

Trifles light as air often suggest to the thinking mind ideas which have revolutionized the world.

A famous ruby was offered to the English government. The report of the crown jeweler was that it was the finest he had ever seen or heard of, but that one of the "facets" was slightly fractured. That invisible fracture reduced the value of the ruby thousands of dollars, and it was rejected from the regalia of England.

It was steady a little thing for the janitor to leave a lamp swinging in the cathedral at Pisa, but in that swaying motion the boy Galileo saw the pendulum, and conceived the idea of thus measuring time.

"I was singing to the mouthpiece of a telephone," said Edison, "when the vibrations of my voice caused a fine steel point to pierce one of my fingers held just behind it. That set me to thinking. If I could record the motions of the point and send it over the same surface afterward, I saw no reason why the thing would not talk. I determined to make a machine that would work accurately, and gave my assistants the necessary instructions, telling them what I had discovered. That's the whole story. The phonograph is the result of the pricking of a finger."

It was a little thing for a cow to kick over a lantern left in a shanty, but it laid Chicago in ashes, and rendered homeless a hundred thousand people.

Some little weakness, some self-indulgence, a quick temper, want of decision, are little things, you say, when placed beside great abilities, but they have wrecked many a career.

The Parliament of Great Britain, the Congress of the United States, and representative governments all over the world have come from King John signing the Magna Carta.

Bentham says, "The turn of a sentence has decided many a friendship, and, for aught we know, the fate of many a kingdom."

Perhaps you turned a cold shoulder but once, and made but one stinging remark, yet it may have cost you a friend forever.

The sight of a stranded cuttlefish led Cuvier to an investigation which made him one of the greatest natural historians in the world. The web of a spider suggested to Captain Brown the idea of a suspension bridge.

A missing marriage certificate kept the hod carrier of Hugh Miller from establishing his claim to the Earldom of Crawford. The masons would call out, "John, Yearl of Crawford, bring us *anither hod o' lime.*"

The absence of a comma in a bill which passed through Congress years ago cost our government a million dollars. A single misspelled word prevented a deserving young man from obtaining a situation as instructor in a New England college.

"I cannot see that you have made any progress since my last visit," said a gentleman to Michael Angelo. "But," said the sculptor, "I have retouched this part, polished that, softened that feature, brought out that muscle, given some expression to this lip, more energy to that limb, etc." "But they are trifles!" exclaimed the visitor. "It may be so," replied the great artist, "but trifles make perfection, and perfection is no trifle." That infinite patience which made Michael Angelo spend a week in bringing out a muscle in a statue, with more vital fidelity to truth, or Gerrit Dou a day in giving the right effect to a dewdrop on a cabbage leaf, makes all the difference between success and failure.

The cry of the infant Moses attracted the attention of Pharoah's daughter, and gave the Jews a lawgiver. A bird alighting on the bough of a tree at the mouth of the cave where Mahomet lay hid turned aside his pursuers, and gave a prophet to many nations. A flight of birds probably prevented Columbus from discovering this continent. When he was growing anxious, Martin Alonzo Pinzon persuaded him to follow a flight of parrots toward the southwest; for to the Spanish seamen of that day it was good luck to follow in the wake of a flock of birds when on a voyage of discovery. But for his change of course Columbus would have reached the coast of Florida. "Never," wrote Humboldt, "had the flight of birds more important consequences."

The children of a spectacle maker placed two or more pairs of the spectacles before each other in play and told their father that distant objects looked larger. From this hint came the telescope.

Every day is a little life; and our whole life but a day repeated. Those that dare lose a day are dangerously prodigal; those that dare misspend it, desperate. What is the happiness of your life made up of? Little courtesies, little kindnesses, pleasant words, genial smiles, a friendly letter, good wishes, and good deeds. One in a million—once in a lifetime—may do a heroic action.

Napoleon was a master of trifles. To details which his inferior officers thought too microscopic for their notice he gave the most exhaustive consideration. Nothing was too small for his attention. He must know all about the provisions, the horse fodder, the biscuits, the camp kettles, the shoes. When the bugle sounded for the march to battle, every officer had his orders as to the exact route which he should follow, the exact day he was to arrive at a certain station, and the exact hour he was to leave, and they were all to reach the point of destination at a precise moment.

It is said that nothing could be more perfectly planned than his memorable march which led to the victory of Austerlitz, and which sealed the fate of Europe for many years. He would often charge his absent officers to send him perfectly accurate returns, even to the smallest detail. "When they are sent to me, I give up every occupation in order to read them in detail, and to observe the difference between one monthly return and another. No young girl enjoys her novel as much as I do these returns." Napoleon left nothing to chance, nothing to contingency, so far as he could possibly avoid it. Everything was planned to a nicety before he attempted to execute it.

Wellington, too, was "great in little things." He knew no such things as trifles. While other generals trusted to subordinates, he gave his personal attention to the minutest detail. The history of many a failure could be written in three words, "Lack of detail." How many a lawyer has failed from the lack of details in deeds and important papers, the lack of little words which seemed like surplusage, and which involved his clients in litigation, and often great losses! How many wills are contested from the carelessness of lawyers in the omission or shading of words, or ambiguous use of language!

Not even Helen of Troy, it is said, was beautiful enough to spare the tip of her nose; and if Cleopatra's had been an inch shorter Mark Antony might never have become infatuated with her wonderful charms, and the blemish would have changed the history of the world. Anne Boleyn's fascinating smile split the great Church of Rome in twain, and gave a nation an altered destiny. Napoleon, who feared not to attack the proudest monarchs in their capitols, shrank from the political influence of one independent woman in private life, Madame de Staël.

Cromwell was about to sail for America when a law was passed prohibiting emigration. At that time, he was a profligate, having squandered all his property. But when he found that he could not leave England he reformed his life. Had he not been detained, who can tell what the history of Great Britain would have been?

From the careful and persistent accumulation of innumerable facts, each trivial in itself, but in the aggregate forming a mass of evidence, a Darwin extracts his law of evolution, and a Linnaeus constructs the science of botany. A pan of water and two thermometers were the tools by which Dr. Black discovered latent heat; and a prism, a lens, and a sheet of pasteboard enabled Newton to unfold the composition of light and the origin of colors. An eminent foreign savant called on Dr. Wollaston, and asked to be shown over those laboratories of his in which science had been enriched by so many great discoveries, when the doctor took him into a little study, and, pointing to an old tea tray on the table, on which stood a few watch glasses, test papers, a small balance, and a blowpipe, said, "There is my laboratory." A burnt stick and a barn door served David Wilkie in lieu of pencil and paper. A single potato, carried to England by Sir Walter Raleigh in the sixteenth century, has multiplied into food for millions, driving famine from Ireland again and again.

It seemed a small thing to drive William Brewster, John Robinson, and the poor people of Austerfield and Scrooby into perpetual exile, but as Pilgrims they became the founders of a mighty people.

A few immortal sentences from Garrison and Phillips, a few poems from Lowell and Whittier, and the leaven is at work which will not cease its action until the whipping post and bodily servitude are abolished forever.

> *For want of a nail the shoe was lost,*
> *For want of a shoe the horse was lost;*
> *For want of a horse the rider was lost, and all, says*
> *Poor Richard, for want of a horseshoe nail.*

A single remark dropped by an unknown person in the street led to the successful story of *The Bread-Winners*. A hymn chanted by the barefooted friars in the temple of Jupiter at Rome led to the famous *Decline and Fall of the Roman Empire*.

"Words are things" says Byron, "and a small drop of ink, falling like dew upon a thought, produces that which makes thousands, perhaps millions, think."

"I give these books for the founding of a college in this colony"; such were the words of 10 ministers who in the year 1700 assembled at the village of Branford, a few miles east of New Haven. Each of the worthy fathers deposited a few books upon the table around which they were sitting; such was the founding of Yale College.

Great men are noted for their attention to trifles. Goethe once asked a monarch to excuse him, during an interview, while he went to an adjoining room to jot down a stray thought. Hogarth would make sketches of rare faces and characteristics upon his fingernails upon the streets. Indeed, to a truly great mind there are no little things. Trifles light as air suggest to the keen observer the solution of mighty problems. Bits of glass arranged to amuse children led to the discovery of the kaleidoscope. Goodyear discovered how to vulcanize rubber by forgetting, until it became red hot, a skillet containing a compound which he had before considered worthless.

A shipworm boring a piece of wood suggested to Sir Isambard Brunel the idea of a tunnel under the Thames at London. Tracks of extinct animals in the old red sandstone led Hugh Miller on and on until he became the greatest geologist of his time. Sir Walter Scott once saw a shepherd boy plodding sturdily along, and asked him to ride. This boy was George Kemp, who became so enthusiastic in his study of sculpture that he walked 50 miles and back to see a beautiful statue. He did not forget the kindness of Sir Walter, and, when the latter died, threw his soul into the design of the magnificent monument erected in Edinburgh to the memory of the author of *Waverley*.

A poor boy applied for a situation at a bank in Paris but was refused. As he left the door, he picked up a pin. The bank president saw this, called the boy back, and gave him a situation from which he rose until he became the greatest banker of Paris—Jacques Laffitte.

A Massachusetts soldier in the Civil War observed a bird hulling rice, and shot it; taking its bill for a model, he invented a hulling machine which has revolutionized the rice business.

The eye is a perpetual camera imprinting upon the sensitive mental plates and packing away in the brain for future use every face, every tree, every plant, flower, hill, stream, mountain, every scene upon the street, in fact, everything which comes within its range. There is a phonograph in our natures which catches, however thoughtless and transient, every syllable we utter, and registers forever the slightest enunciation, and renders it immortal. These notes may appear a thousand years hence, reproduced in our descendants, in all their beautiful or terrible detail.

"Least of all seeds, greatest of all harvests," seems to be one of the great laws of nature. All life comes from microscopic beginnings. In nature there is nothing small. The microscope reveals as great a world below as the telescope above. All of nature's laws govern the smallest atoms, and a single drop of water is a miniature ocean.

The strength of a chain lies in its weakest link, however large and strong all the others may be. We are all inclined to be proud of our strong points, while we are sensitive and neglectful of our weaknesses. Yet it is our greatest weakness which measures our real strength.

A soldier who escapes the bullets of a thousand battles may die from the scratch of a pin, and many a ship has survived the shocks of icebergs and the storms of ocean only to founder in a smooth sea from holes made by tiny insects.

Small things become great when a great soul sees them. A single noble or heroic act of one man has sometimes elevated a nation. Many an honorable career has resulted from a kind word spoken in season or the warm grasp of a friendly hand.

> *It is the little rift within the lute*
> *That by and by will make the music mute,*
> *And, ever widening, slowly silence all.*

> **—Alfred, Lord Tennyson**

> *It was only a glad 'good-morning,'*
> *As she passed along the way,*
> *But it spread the morning's glory*
> *Over the livelong day.*

> *Only a thought in passing—a smile, or encouraging word,*
> *has lifted many a burden no other gift could have stirred.*

THE SALARY NOT IN YOUR PAY ENVELOPE

The quality which you put into your work will determine the quality of your life. The habit of insisting upon the best of which you are capable, of always demanding of yourself the highest, never accepting the lowest or second best, no matter how small your remuneration, will make all the difference to you between failure and success.

"If the laborer gets no more than the wages his employer offers him, he is cheated; he cheats himself."

A boy or a man who works simply for his salary, and is actuated by no higher motive, is dishonest, and the one whom he most defrauds is himself. He is cheating himself, in the quality of his daily work, of that which all the after years, try as he may, can never give him back.

If I were allowed but one utterance on this subject, so vital to every young man starting on the journey of life, I would say: "Don't think too much of the amount of salary your employer gives you at the start. Think, rather, of the possible salary you can give yourself, in increasing your skill, in expanding your experience, in enlarging and ennobling yourself." A man's or a boy's work is material with which to build character and manhood. It is life's school for practical training of the faculties, stretching the mind, and strengthening and developing the intellect, not a mere mill for grinding out a salary of dollars and cents.

Bismarck was said to have really founded the German Empire when working for a small salary as secretary to the German legation in Russia; for in that position, he absorbed the secrets of strategy and diplomacy which later were used so effectively for his country. He worked so assiduously, so efficiently, that Germany prized his services more than those of the ambassador himself. If Bismarck had earned only his salary, he might have remained a perpetual clerk, and Germany a tangle of petty states.

I have never known an employee to rise rapidly, or even to get beyond mediocrity, whose pay envelope was his goal, who could not see infinitely more in his work than what he found in the envelope on Saturday night. That is necessity; but the larger part of the real pay of a real man's work is outside of the pay envelope.

One part of this outside salary is the opportunity of the employee to absorb the secrets of his employer's success, and to learn from his mistakes, while he is being paid for learning his trade or profession. The other part, and the best of all, is the opportunity for growth, for development, for mental expansion; the opportunity to become a larger, broader, more efficient man.

The opportunity for growth in a disciplinary institution, where the practical faculties, the executive faculties, are brought into systematic, vigorous exercise at a definite time and for a definite number of hours, is an advantage beyond computation. There is no estimating the value of such training. It is the opportunity, my employee friend, that will help you to make a large man of yourself, which, perhaps, you could not possibly do without being employed in some kind of an institution which has the motive, the machinery, the patronage to give you the disciplining and training you need to bring out your strongest qualities. And instead of paying for the opportunity of unfolding and developing from a green, ignorant boy into a strong, level-headed, efficient man, you are paid!

The youth who is always haggling over the question of how many dollars and cents he will sell his services for, little realizes how he is cheating himself by not looking at the larger salary he can pay himself in increasing his skill, in expanding his experience, and in making himself a better, stronger, more useful man.

The few dollars he finds in his pay envelope are to this larger salary as the chips which fly from the sculptor's chisel are to the angel which he is trying to call out of the marble.

You can draw from the faithfulness of your work, from the grand spirit which you bring to it, the high purpose which emanates from you in its performance, a recompense so munificent that what your employer pays you will seem insignificant beside it. He pays you in dollars; you pay yourself in valuable experience, in fine training, in increased efficiency, in splendid discipline, in self-expression, in character building.

Then, too, the ideal employer gives those who work for him a great deal that is not found in the pay envelope. He gives them encouragement, sympathy. He inspires them with the possibility of doing something higher, better.

How small and narrow and really blind to his own interests must be the youth who can weigh a question of salary against all those privileges he receives in exchange for the meager services he is able to render his employer.

Do not fear that your employer will not recognize your merit and advance you as rapidly as you deserve. It he is looking for efficient employees—and what employer is not? —it will be to his own interest to do so—just as soon as it is profitable. W. Bourke Cockran, himself a remarkable example of success, says: "The man who brings to his occupation a loyal desire to do his best is certain to succeed. By doing the thing at hand surpassingly well, he shows that it would be profitable to employ him in some higher form of occupation, and, when there is profit in his promotion, he is pretty sure to secure it."

Do you think that kings of business like Andrew Carnegie, John Wanamaker, Robert C. Ogden, and other lesser powers in the commercial world would have attained their present commanding success had they hesitated and haggled about a dollar or two of salary when they began their lifework? If they had, they would now probably be working on comparatively small salaries for other people. It was not salary, but opportunity, that each wanted—a chance to show what was in him, to absorb the secrets of the business. They were satisfied with a dollar or two apiece a week, hardly enough to live on, while they were learning the lessons that made them what they are today. No, the boys who rise in the world are not those who, at the start, split hairs about salaries.

Often, we see bright boys who have worked, perhaps for years, on small salaries, suddenly jumping, as if by magic, into high and responsible positions. Why? Simply because, while their employers were paying them but a few dollars a week, they were paying themselves vastly more in the fine quality of their work, in the enthusiasm, determination, and high purpose they brought to their tasks, and in increased insight into business methods.

Colonel Robert C. Clowry, president of the Western Union Telegraph Company, worked without pay as a messenger boy for months for experience, which he regarded as worth infinitely more than salary—and scores of our most successful men have cheerfully done the same thing.

A millionaire merchant of New York told me the story of his rise. "I walked from my home in New England to New York," he said, "where I secured a place to sweep out a store for three dollars and a half a week. At the end of a year, I accepted an offer from the firm to remain for five years at a salary of seven dollars and a half a week. Long before this time had expired, however, I had a proposition from another large concern in New York to act as its foreign representative at a salary of 3,000 dollars a year. I told the manager that I was then under contract, but that, when my time should be completed, I should be glad to talk with him in regard to his proposition." When his contract was nearly up, he was called into the office of the head of the house, and a new contract with him for a term of years at 3,000 dollars a year was proposed.

The young man told his employers that the manager of another house had offered him that amount a year or more before, but that he did not accept it because he wouldn't break his contract. They told him they would think the matter over and see what they could do for him. Incredible as it may seem, they notified him, a little later, that they were prepared to enter into a ten-year contract with him at 10,000 dollars a year, and the contract was closed. He told me that he and his wife lived on eight dollars a week in New York, during a large part of this time, and that, by saving and investments, they laid up $117,000. At the end of his contract, he was taken into the firm as a partner, and became a millionaire.

Suppose that this boy had listened to his associates, who probably said to him, many times: "What a fool you are, George, to work here overtime to do the things which others neglect! Why should you stay here nights and help pack goods, and all that sort of thing, when it is not expected of you?" Would he then have risen above them, leaving them in the ranks of perpetual employees? No, but the boy who walked 100 miles to New York to get a job saw in every opportunity a great occasion, for he could not tell when fate might be taking his measure for a larger place.

The very first time he swept out the store, he felt within him the ability to become a great merchant, and he determined that he would be. He felt that the opportunity was the salary. The chance actually to do with his own hands the thing which he wanted to learn; to see the way in which princely merchants do business; to watch their methods; to absorb their processes; to make their secrets his own—this was his salary, compared with which the three dollars and fifty cents looked contemptible. He put himself into training, always looking out for the main chance. He never allowed anything of importance to escape his attention. When he was not working, he was watching others, studying methods, and asking questions of everybody he came in contact with in the store, so eager was he to learn how everything was done. He told me that he did not go out of New York City for 12 years; that he preferred to study the store, and to absorb every bit of knowledge that he could, for he was bound someday to be a partner or to have a store of his own.

It is not difficult to see a proprietor in the boy who sweeps the store or waits on customers—if the qualities that make a proprietor are in him—by watching him work for a single day. You can tell by the spirit which he brings to his task whether there is in him the capacity for growth, expansion, enlargement; an ambition to rise, to be somebody, or an inclination to shirk, to do as little as possible for the largest amount of salary.

When you get a job, just think of yourself as actually starting out in business for yourself, as really working for yourself. Get as much salary as you can, but remember that that is a very small part of the consideration. You have actually gotten an opportunity to get right into the very heart of the great activities of a large concern, to get close to men who do things; an opportunity to absorb knowledge and valuable secrets on every hand; an opportunity to drink in, through your eyes and your ears, knowledge wherever you go in the establishment, knowledge that will be invaluable to you in the future.

Every hint and every suggestion which you can pick up, every bit of knowledge you can absorb, you should regard as a part of your future capital which will be worth more than money capital when you start out for yourself.

Just make up your mind that you are going to be a sponge in that institution and absorb every particle of information and knowledge possible.

Resolve that you will call upon all of your resourcefulness, your inventiveness, your ingenuity, to devise new and better ways of doing things; that you will be progressive, up-to-date; that you will enter into your work with a spirit of enthusiasm and a zest which know no bounds, and you will be surprised to see how quickly you will attract the attention of those above you.

This striving for excellence will make you grow. It will call out your resources, call out the best thing in you. The constant stretching of the mind over problems which interest you, which are to mean everything to you in the future, will help you expand into a broader, larger, more effective man.

If you work with this spirit, you will form a like habit of accuracy, of close observation; a habit of reading human nature; a habit of adjusting means to ends; a habit of thoroughness, of system; a habit of putting your best into everything you do, which means the ultimate attainment of your maximum efficiency. In other words, if you give your best to your employer, the best possible comes back to you in skill, training, shrewdness, acumen, and power.

Your employer may pinch you on salary, but he cannot close your eyes and ears; he cannot shut off your perceptive faculties; he cannot keep you from absorbing the secrets of his business which may have been purchased by him at an enormous cost of toil and sacrifice and even of several failures.

On the other hand, it is impossible for you to rob your employer by clipping your hours, shirking your work, by carelessness or indifference, without robbing yourself of infinitely more, of capital which is worth vastly more than money capital—the chance to make a man of yourself, the chance to have a clean record behind you instead of a smirched one.

If you think you are being kept back, if you are working for too small a salary, if favoritism puts someone into a position above you which you have justly earned, never mind, no one can rob you of your greatest reward, the skill, the efficiency, the power you have gained, the consciousness of doing your level best, of giving the best thing in you to your employer, all of which advantages you will carry with you to your next position, whatever it may be.

Don't say to yourself, "I am not paid for doing this extra work; I do not get enough salary, anyway, and it is perfectly right for me to shirk when my employer is not in sight or to clip my hours when I can," for this means a loss of self-respect. You will never again have the same confidence in your ability to succeed; you will always be conscious that you have done a little, mean thing, and no amount of juggling with yourself can induce that inward monitor which says "right" to the well-done thing and "wrong" to the botched work, to alter its verdict in your favor.

There is something within you that you cannot bribe; a divine sense of justice and right that cannot be blindfolded. Nothing will ever compensate you for the loss of faith in yourself. You may still succeed when others have lost confidence in you, but never when you have lost confidence in yourself. If you do not respect yourself; if you do not believe in yourself, your career is at an end so far as its upward tendency is concerned.

Then again, an employee's reputation is his capital. In the absence of money capital, his reputation means everything. It not only follows him around from one employer to another, but it also follows him when he goes into business for himself, and is always either helping or hindering him, according to its nature.

Contrast the condition of a young man starting out for himself who has looked upon his position as a sacred trust, a great opportunity, backed, buttressed, and supported by a splendid past, an untarnished reputation—a reputation for being a dead-in-earnest hard worker, square, loyal, and true to his employer's interests—with that of another young man of equal ability starting out for himself, who has done just as little work for his salary as possible, and who has gone on the principle that the more he could get out of an employer—the more salary he could get with less effort—the shrewder, smarter man he was.

The very reputation of the first young man is splendid credit. He is backed up by the good opinion of everybody that knows him. People are afraid of the other: they cannot trust him. He beat his employer, why should not he beat others? Everybody knows that he has not been honest at heart with his employer, not loyal or true. He must work all the harder to overcome the handicap of a bad reputation, a smirched record.

In other words, he is starting out in life with a heavy handicap, which, if it does not drag him down to failure, will make his burden infinitely greater, and success, even a purely commercial success, so much the harder to attain.

There is nothing like a good, solid, substantial reputation, a clean record, an untarnished past. It sticks to us through life, and is always helping us. We find it waiting at the bank when we try to borrow money, or at the jobber's when we ask for credit. It is always backing us up and helping us in all sorts of ways.

Young men are sometimes surprised at their rapid advancement. They cannot understand it, because they do not realize the tremendous power of a clean name, of a good reputation which is backing them.

I know a young man who came to New York, got a position in a publishing house at 15 dollars a week, and worked 5 years before he received 35 dollars a week.

The other employees and his friends called him a fool for staying at the office after hours and taking work home nights and holidays, for such a small salary; but he told them that the opportunity was what he was after, not the salary.

His work attracted the attention of a publisher who offered him 60 dollars a week, and very soon advanced him to 75; but he carried with him to the new position the same habits of painstaking, hard work, never thinking of the salary, but regarding the opportunity as everything.

Employees sometimes think that they get no credit for trying to do more than they are paid for; but here is an instance of a young man who attracted the attention of others even outside of the firm he worked for, just because he was trying to earn a great deal more than he was paid for doing.

The result was that in less than two years from the time he was receiving 60 dollars a week, he went to a third large publishing house at 10,000 dollars a year, and also with an interest in the business.

The salary is of very little importance to you in comparison with the reputation for integrity and efficiency you have left behind you and the experience you have gained while earning the salary. These are the great things.

In olden times boys had to give years of their time in order to learn a trade, and often would pay their employer for the opportunity. English boys used to think it was a great opportunity to be able to get into a good concern, with a chance to work without salary for years in order to learn their business or trade. Now the boy is paid for learning his trade.

Many employees may not think it is so very bad to clip their hours, to shirk at every opportunity, to sneak away and hide during business hours, to loiter when out on business for their employer, to go to their work in the morning all used up from dissipation; but often when they try to get another place their reputation has gone before them, and they are not wanted.

Others excuse themselves for poor work on the ground that their employer does not appreciate their services and is mean to them. A youth might just as well excuse himself for his boorish manners and ungentlemanly conduct on the ground that other people were mean and ungentlemanly to him.

My young friends, you have nothing to do with your employer's character or his method of doing things. You may not be able to make him do what is right, but you can do right yourself. You may not be able to make him a gentleman, but you can be one yourself; and you cannot afford to ruin yourself and your whole future just because your employer is not what he ought to be. No matter how mean and stingy he may be, your opportunity for the time is with him, and it rests with you whether you will use it or abuse it, whether you will make of it a stepping stone or a stumbling block.

The fact is that your present position, your way of doing your work, is the key that will unlock the door above you. Slighted work, botched work, will never make a key to unlock the door to anything but failure and disgrace.

There is nothing else so valuable to you as an opportunity to build a name for yourself. Your reputation is the foundation for your future success, and if you slip rotten hours, and slighted, botched work into the foundation, your superstructure will topple. The foundation must be clean, solid, and firm.

The quality which you put into your work will determine the quality of your life. The habit of insisting upon the best of which you are capable, of always demanding of yourself the highest, never accepting the lowest or second best, no matter how small your remuneration, will make all the difference to you between mediocrity or failure, and success.

If you bring to your work the spirit of an artist instead of an artisan, a burning zeal, an absorbing enthusiasm, these will take the drudgery out of it and make it a delight.

Take no chances of marring your reputation by the picayune and unworthy endeavor "to get square" with a stingy or mean employer. Never mind what kind of a man he is, resolve that you will approach your task in the spirit of a master, that whether he is a man of high ideals or not, you will be one. Remember that you are a sculptor and that every act is a chisel blow upon life's marble block. You cannot afford to strike false blows which may mar the angel that sleeps in the stone. Whether it is beautiful or hideous, divine or brutal, the image you evolve from the block must stand as an expression of yourself, of your ideals.

Those who do not care how they do their work, if they can only get through with it and get their salary for it, pay very dearly for their trifling; they cut very sorry figures in life. Regard your work as a great life school for the broadening, deepening, rounding into symmetry, harmony, beauty, of your God-given faculties, which are uncut diamonds sacredly entrusted to you for the polishing and bringing out of their hidden wealth and beauty. Look upon it as a man builder, a character builder, and not as a mere living getter. Regard the living-getting, moneymaking part of your career as a mere incidental as compared with the man-making part of it.

The smallest people in the world are those who work for salary alone. The little money you get in your pay envelope is a pretty small, low motive for which to work. It may be necessary to secure your bread and butter, but you have something infinitely higher to satisfy than that; that is, your sense of the right; the demand in you to do your level best, to be a man, to do the square thing, the fair thing. These should speak so loud in you that the mere bread-and-butter question will be insignificant in comparison.

Many young employees, just because they do not get quite as much salary as they think they should, deliberately throw away all of the other, larger, grander remuneration possible for them outside of their pay envelope, for the sake of "getting square" with their employer. They deliberately adopt a shirking, do-as-little-as-possible policy, and instead of getting this larger, more important salary, which they can pay themselves, they prefer the consequent arrested development, and become small, narrow, inefficient, rutty men and women, with nothing large or magnanimous, nothing broad, noble, progressive in their nature. Their leadership faculties, their initiative, their planning ability, their ingenuity and resourcefulness, inventiveness, and all the qualities which make the leader, the large, full, complete man, remain undeveloped. While trying to "get square" with their employer, by giving him pinched service, they blight their own growth, strangle their own prospects, and go through life half men instead of full men—small, narrow, weak men, instead of the strong, grand, complete men they might be.

I have known employees actually to work harder in scheming, shirking, trying to keep from working hard in the performance of their duties than they would have worked if they had tried to do their best, and had given the largest, the most liberal service possible to their employers. The hardest work in the world is that which is grudgingly done.

Start out with a tacit understanding with yourself that you will be a man, that you will express in your work the highest thing in you, the best thing in you. You cannot afford to debase or demoralize yourself by bringing out your mean side, the lowest and most despicable thing in you.

Never mind whether your employer appreciates the high quality of your work or not, or thinks more of you for your conscientiousness, you will certainly think more of yourself after getting the approval of that still small voice within you which says "right" to the noble act. The effort always to do your best will enlarge your capacity for doing things, and will encourage you to push ahead toward larger triumphs.

Everywhere we see people who are haunted by the ghosts of half-finished jobs, the dishonest work done away back in their youth. These covered-up defects are always coming back to humiliate them later, to trip them up, and to bar their progress. The great failure army is full of people who have tried to get square with their employers for the small salary and lack of appreciation.

No one can respect himself or have that sublime faith in himself which makes for high achievement while he puts half-hearted, mean service into his work. The man who has not learned to fling his whole soul into his task, who has not learned the secret of taking the drudgery out of his work by putting the best of himself into it, has not learned the first principles of success or happiness. Let other people do the poor jobs, the botched work, if they will. Keep your standard up. It is a lofty ideal that redeems the life from the curse of commonness and imparts a touch of nobility to the personality.

No matter how small your salary, or how unappreciative your employer, bring the entire man to your task; be all there; fling your life into it with all the energy and enthusiasm you can muster. Poor work injures your employer a little, but it may ruin you. Be proud of your work and go to it every morning superbly equipped; go to it in the spirit of a master, of a conqueror. Determine to do your level best and never to demoralize yourself by doing your second best.

Conduct yourself in such a way that you can always look yourself in the face without wincing; then you will have a courage born of conviction, of personal nobility and integrity which have never been tarnished.

What your employer thinks of you, what the world thinks of you, is not half as important as what you think of yourself. Others are with you comparatively little through life. You have to live with yourself day and night through your whole existence, and you cannot afford to tie that divine thing in you to a scoundrel.

Chapter
43

EXPECT GREAT THINGS
OF YOURSELF

"Why," asked Mirabeau, "should we call ourselves men, unless it be to succeed in everything everywhere?" Nothing else will so nerve you to accomplish great things as to believe in your own greatness, in your own marvelous possibilities. Count that man an enemy who shakes your faith in yourself, in your ability to do the thing you have set your heart upon doing, for when your confidence is gone, your power is gone. Your achievement will never rise higher than your self-faith. It would be as reasonable for Napoleon to have expected to get his army over the Alps by sitting down and declaring that the undertaking was too great for him, as for you to hope to achieve anything significant in life while harboring grave doubts and fears as to your ability.

The miracles of civilization have been performed by men and women of great self-confidence, who had unwavering faith in their power to accomplish the tasks they undertook. The race would have been centuries behind what it is today had it not been for their grit, their determination, their persistence in finding and making real the thing they believed in and which the world often denounced as chimerical or impossible.

There is no law by which you can achieve success in anything without expecting it, demanding it, assuming it. There must be a strong, firm self-faith first, or the thing will never come. There is no room for chance in God's world of system and supreme order. Everything must have not only a cause, but a sufficient cause—a cause as large as the result. A stream cannot rise higher than its source. A great success must have a great source in expectation, in self-confidence, and in persistent endeavor to attain it. No matter how great the ability, how large the genius, or how splendid the education, the achievement will never rise higher than the confidence. He can who thinks he can, and he can't who thinks he can't. This is an inexorable, indisputable law.

It does not matter what other people think of you, of your plans, or of your aims. No matter if they call you a visionary, a crank, or a dreamer; you must believe in yourself. You forsake yourself when you lose your confidence. Never allow anybody or any misfortune to shake your belief in yourself. You may lose your property, your health, your reputation, other people's confidence, even; but there is always hope for you so long as you keep a firm faith in yourself. If you never lose that, but keep pushing on, the world will, sooner or later, make way for you.

A soldier once took a message to Napoleon in such great haste that the horse he rode dropped dead before he delivered the paper. Napoleon dictated his answer and, handing it to the messenger, ordered him to mount his own horse and deliver it with all possible speed.

The messenger looked at the magnificent animal, with its superb trappings, and said, "Nay, General, but this is too gorgeous, too magnificent for a common soldier."

Napoleon said, "Nothing is too good or too magnificent for a French soldier."

The world is full of people like this poor French soldier, who think that what others have is too good for them; that it does not fit their humble condition; that they are not expected to have as good things as those who are "more favored." They do not realize how they weaken themselves by this mental attitude of self-depreciation or self-effacement. They do not claim enough, expect enough, or demand enough of or for themselves.

You will never become a giant if you only make a pygmy's claim for yourself; if you only expect small things of yourself. There is no law which can cause a pygmy's thinking to produce a giant. The statue follows the model. The model is the inward vision.

Most people have been educated to think that it was not intended they should have the best there is in the world; that the good and the beautiful things of life were not designed for them, but were reserved for those especially favored by fortune. They have grown up under this conviction of their inferiority, and of course they will be inferior until they claim superiority as their birthright. A vast number of men and women who are really capable of doing great things, do small things, live mediocre lives, because they do not expect or demand enough of themselves. They do not know how to call out their best.

One reason why the human race as a whole has not measured up to its possibilities, to its promise; one reason why we see everywhere splendid ability doing the work of mediocrity; is because people do not think half enough of themselves. We do not realize our divinity; that we are a part of the great causation principle of the universe.

We do not think highly enough of our superb birthright, nor comprehend to what heights of sublimity we were intended and expected to rise, nor to what extent we can really be masters of ourselves. We fail to see that we can control our own destiny: make ourselves do whatever is possible; make ourselves become whatever we long to be.

"If we choose to be no more than clods of clay," says Marie Corelli, "then we shall be used as clods of clay for braver feet to tread on."

The persistent thought that you are not as good as others, that you are a weak, ineffective being, will lower your whole standard of life and paralyze your ability.

A man who is self-reliant, positive, optimistic, and undertakes his work with the assurance of success, magnetizes conditions. He draws to himself the literal fulfilment of the promise, *"For unto every one that hath shall be given, and he shall have abundance." (Matthew 25:29a)*

There is everything in assuming the part we wish to play and playing it royally. If you are ambitious to do big things, you must make a large program for yourself, and assume the part it demands.

There is something in the atmosphere of the man who has a large and true estimate of himself, who believes that he is going to win out; something in his very appearance that wins half the battle before a blow is struck. Things get out of the way of the vigorous, affirmative man, which are always tripping the self-depreciating, negative man.

We often hear it said of a man, "Everything he undertakes succeeds," or "Everything he touches turns to gold." By the force of his character and the creative power of his thought, such a man wrings success from the most adverse circumstances. Confidence begets confidence. A man who carries in his very presence an air of victory, radiates assurance, and imparts to others confidence that he can do the thing he attempts. As time goes on, he is reenforced not only by the power of his own thought, but also by that of all who know him. His friends and acquaintances affirm and reaffirm his ability to succeed, and make each successive triumph easier of achievement than its predecessor. His self-poise, assurance, confidence, and ability increase in a direct ratio to the number of his achievements.

As the savage Indian thought that the power of every enemy he conquered entered into himself, so in reality does every conquest in war, in peaceful industry, in commerce, in invention, in science, or in art add to the conqueror's power to do the next thing.

Set the mind toward the thing you would accomplish so resolutely, so definitely, and with such vigorous determination, and put so much grit into your resolution, that nothing on earth can turn you from your purpose until you attain it.

This very assertion of superiority, the assumption of power, the affirmation of belief in yourself, the mental attitude that claims success as an inalienable birthright, will strengthen the whole man and give power to a combination of faculties which doubt, fear, and a lack of confidence undermine.

Confidence is the Napoleon of the mental army. It doubles and trebles the power of all the other faculties. The whole mental army waits until confidence leads the way.

Even a racehorse cannot win the prize after it has once lost confidence in itself. Courage, born of self-confidence, is the prod which brings out the last ounce of reserve force.

The reason why so many men fail is because they do not commit themselves with a determination to win at any cost. They do not have that superb confidence in themselves which never looks back; which burns all bridges behind it. There is just uncertainty enough as to whether they will succeed to take the edge off their effort, and it is just this little difference between doing pretty well and flinging all oneself, all his power, into his career, that makes the difference between mediocrity and a grand achievement.

If you doubt your ability to do what you set out to do; if you think that others are better fitted to do it than you; if you fear to let yourself out and take chances; if you lack boldness; if you have a timid, shrinking nature; if the negatives preponderate in your vocabulary; if you think that you lack positiveness, initiative, aggressiveness, ability; you can never win anything very great until you change your whole mental attitude and learn to have great faith in yourself. Fear, doubt, and timidity must be turned out of your mind.

Your own mental picture of yourself is a good measure of yourself and your possibilities. If there is no outreach to your mind, no spirit of daring, no firm self-faith, you will never accomplish much.

A man's confidence measures the height of his possibilities. A stream cannot rise higher than its fountainhead.

Power is largely a question of strong, vigorous, perpetual thinking along the line of the ambition, parallel with the aim—the great life purpose. Here is where power originates.

The deed must first live in the thought or it will never be a reality; and a strong, vigorous concept of the thing we want to do is a tremendous initial step. A thought that is timidly born will be timidly executed. There must be vigor of conception or an indifferent execution.

All the greatest achievements in the world began in longing—in dreamings and hopings which for a time were nursed in despair, with no light in sight. This longing kept the courage up and made self-sacrifice easier until the thing dreamed of—the mental vision—was realized.

"According to your faith be it unto you." (Matthew 9:29b) Our faith is a very good measure of what we get out of life. The man of weak faith gets little; the man of mighty faith gets much.

The very intensity of your confidence in your ability to do the thing you attempt is definitely related to the degree of your achievement.

If we were to analyze the marvelous successes of many of our self-made men, we should find that when they first started out in active life, they held the confident, vigorous, persistent thought of and belief in their ability to accomplish what they had undertaken. Their mental attitude was set so stubbornly toward their goal that the doubts and fears which dog and hinder and frighten the man who holds a low estimate of himself, who asks, demands, and expects but little, of or for himself, got out of their path, and the world made way for them.

We are very apt to think of men who have been unusually successful in any line as greatly favored by fortune; and we try to account for it in all sorts of ways but the right one. The fact is that their success represents their expectations of themselves—the sum of their creative, positive, habitual thinking. It is their mental attitude outpictured and made tangible in their environment. They have wrought—created— what they have and what they are out of their constructive thought and their unquenchable faith in themselves.

We must not only believe we can succeed, but we must believe it with all our hearts.

We must have a positive conviction that we can attain success.

No lukewarm energy or indifferent ambition ever accomplished anything. There must be vigor in our expectation, in our faith, in our determination, in our endeavor. We must resolve with the energy that does things.

Not only must the desire for the thing we long for be kept uppermost, but there must be strongly concentrated intensity of effort to attain our object.

As it is the fierceness of the heat that melts the iron ore and makes it possible to weld it or mold it into shape; as it is the intensity of the electrical force that dissolves the diamond—the hardest known substance; so, it is the concentrated aim, the invincible purpose, that wins success. Nothing was ever accomplished by a half-hearted desire.

Many people make a very poor showing in life, because there is no vim, no vigor in their efforts. Their resolutions are spineless; there is no backbone in their endeavor—no grit in their ambition.

One must have that determination which never looks back and which knows no defeat; that resolution which burns all bridges behind it and is willing to risk everything upon the effort. When a man ceases to believe in himself—gives up the fight—you cannot do much for him except to try to restore what he has lost—his self-faith—and to get out of his head the idea that there is a fate which tosses him hither and thither, a mysterious destiny which decides things whether he will or not. You cannot do much with him until he comprehends that he is bigger than any fate; that he has within himself a power mightier than any force outside of him.

One reason why the careers of most of us are so pinched and narrow, is because we do not have a large faith in ourselves and in our power to accomplish. We are held back by too much caution. We are timid about venturing. We are not bold enough.

Whatever we long for, yearn for, struggle for, and hold persistently in the mind, we tend to become just in exact proportion to the intensity and persistence of the thought. We think ourselves into smallness, into inferiority by thinking downward. We ought to think upward, then we would reach the heights where superiority dwells. The man whose mind is set firmly toward achievement does not appropriate success, he is success.

Self-confidence is not egotism. It is knowledge, and it comes from the consciousness of possessing the ability requisite for what one undertakes. Civilization today rests upon self-confidence.

A firm self-faith helps a man to project himself with a force that is almost irresistible. A balancer, a doubter, has no projectile power. If he starts at all, he moves with uncertainty. There is no vigor in his initiative, no positiveness in his energy.

There is a great difference between a man who thinks that "perhaps" he can do, or who "will try" to do a thing, and a man who "knows" he can do it, who is "bound" to do it; who feels within himself a pulsating power, an irresistible force, equal to any emergency.

This difference between uncertainty and certainty, between vacillation and decision, between the man who wavers and the man who decides things, between "I hope to" and "I can," between "I'll try" and "I will"— this little difference measures the distance between weakness and power, between mediocrity and excellence, between commonness and superiority.

The man who does things must be able to project himself with a mighty force, to fling the whole weight of his being into his work, ever gathering momentum against the obstacles which confront him; every issue must be met wholly, unhesitatingly. He cannot do this with a wavering, doubting, unstable mind.

The fact that a man believes implicitly that he can do what may seem impossible or very difficult to others, shows that there is something within him that makes him equal to the work he has undertaken.

Faith unites man with the Infinite, and no one can accomplish great things in life unless he works in oneness with the Infinite. When a man lives so near to the Supreme that the divine Presence is felt all the time, then he is in a position to express power.

There is nothing which will multiply one's ability like self-faith. It can make a one-talent man a success, while a ten-talent man without it would fail.

Faith walks on the mountain tops, hence its superior vision. It sees what is invisible to those who follow in the valleys.

It was the sustaining power of a mighty self-faith that enabled Columbus to bear the jeers and imputations of the Spanish cabinet; that sustained him when his sailors were in mutiny and he was at their mercy in a little vessel on an unknown sea; that enabled him to hold steadily to his purpose, entering in his diary day after day—"This day we sailed west, which was our course."

It was this self-faith which gave courage and determination to Fulton to attempt his first trip up the Hudson in the *Clermont*, before thousands of his fellow citizens, who had gathered to howl and jeer at his expected failure. He believed he could do the thing he attempted though the whole world was against him.

What miracles self-confidence has wrought! What impossible deeds it has helped to perform! It took Dewey past cannons, torpedoes, and mines to victory at Manila Bay; it carried Farragut, lashed to the rigging, past the defenses of the enemy in Mobile Bay; it led Nelson and Grant to victory; it has been the great tonic in the world of invention, discovery, and art; it has won a thousand triumphs in war and science which were deemed impossible by doubters and the fainthearted.

Self-faith has been the miracle worker of the ages. It has enabled the inventor and the discoverer to go on and on amidst troubles and trials which otherwise would have utterly disheartened them. It has held innumerable heroes to their tasks until the glorious deeds were accomplished.

The only inferiority in us is what we put into ourselves. If only we better understood our divinity, we should all have this larger faith which is the distinction of the brave soul. We think ourselves into smallness. Were we to think upward we should reach the heights where superiority dwells.

Perhaps there is no other one thing which keeps so many people back as their low estimate of themselves. They are more handicapped by their limiting thought, by their foolish convictions of inefficiency, than by almost anything else, for there is no power in the universe that can help a man do a thing when he thinks he cannot do it. Self-faith must lead the way. You cannot go beyond the limits you set for yourself.

It is one of the most difficult things to a mortal to really believe in his own bigness, in his own grandeur; to believe that his yearnings and hungerings and aspirations for higher, nobler things have any basis in reality or any real, ultimate end. But they are, in fact, the signs of ability to match them, of power to make them real. They are the stirrings of the divinity within us; the call to something better, to go higher.

No man gets very far in the world or expresses great power until self-faith is born in him; until he catches a glimpse of his higher, nobler self; until he realizes that his ambition, his aspiration, are proofs of his ability to reach the ideal which haunts him. The Creator would not have mocked us with the yearning for infinite achievement without giving us the ability and the opportunity for realizing it, any more than he would have mocked the wild birds with an instinct to fly south in the winter without giving them a sunny South to match the instinct.

The cause of whatever comes to you in life is within you. There is where it is created. The thing you long for and work for comes to you because your thought has created it; because there is something inside you that attracts it. It comes because there is an affinity within you for it. Your own comes to you; is always seeking you.

Whenever you see a person who has been unusually successful in any field, remember that he has usually thought himself into his position; his mental attitude and energy have created it; what he stands for in his community has come from his attitude toward life, toward his fellow men, toward his vocation, toward himself. Above all else, it is the outcome of his self-faith, of his inward vision of himself; the result of his estimate of his powers and possibilities.

The men who have done the great things in the world have been profound believers in themselves.

If I could give the young people of America but one word of advice, it would be this: "Believe in yourself with all your might." That is, believe that your destiny is inside of you, that there is a power within you which, if awakened, aroused, developed, and matched with honest effort, will not only make a noble man or woman of you, but will also make you successful and happy.

All through the Bible we find emphasized the miracle-working power of faith. Faith in himself indicates that a man has a glimpse of forces within him which either annihilate the obstacles in the way, or make them seem insignificant in comparison with his ability to overcome them.

Faith opens the door that enables us to look into the soul's limitless possibilities and reveals such powers there, such unconquerable forces, that we are not only encouraged to go on, but feel a great consciousness of added power because we have touched omnipotence, and gotten a glimpse of the great source of things.

Faith is that something within us which does not guess, but knows. It knows because it sees what our coarser selves, our animal natures cannot see. It is the prophet within us, the divine messenger appointed to accompany man through life to guide and direct and encourage him. It gives him a glimpse of his possibilities to keep him from losing heart, from quitting his upward life struggle.

Our faith knows because it sees what we cannot see. It sees resources, powers, potencies which our doubts and fears veil from us. Faith is assured, is never afraid, because it sees the way out; sees the solution of its problem. It has dipped in the realms of our finer life our higher and diviner kingdom. All things are possible to him who has faith, because faith sees, recognizes the power that means accomplishment. If we had faith in God and in ourselves, we could remove all mountains of difficulty, and our lives would be one triumphal march to the goal of our ambition.

If we had faith enough, we could cure all our ills and accomplish the maximum of our possibilities.

Faith never fails; it is a miracle worker. It looks beyond all boundaries, transcends all limitations, penetrates all obstacles and sees the goal.

It is doubt and fear, timidity and cowardice, that hold us down and keep us in mediocrity—doing petty things when we are capable of sublime deeds.

If we had faith enough, we should travel Godward infinitely faster than we do.

The time will come when every human being will have unbounded faith and will live the life triumphant. Then there will be no poverty in the world, no failures, and the discords of life will all vanish.

THE NEXT TIME YOU THINK YOU'RE A FAILURE

If you made a botch of last year, if you feel that it was a failure, that you floundered and blundered and did a lot of foolish things; if you were gullible, made imprudent investments, wasted your time and money, don't drag these ghosts along with you to handicap you and destroy your happiness all through the future.

Haven't you wasted enough energy worrying over what cannot be helped? Don't let these things sap any more of your vitality, waste any more of your time or destroy any more of your happiness.

There is only one thing to do with bitter experiences, blunders and unfortunate mistakes, or with memories that worry us and which kill our efficiency, and that is to forget them, bury them!

Today is a good time to "leave the low-vaulted past," to drop the yesterdays, to forget bitter memories.

Resolve that you will close the door on everything in the past that pains and cannot help you. Free yourself from everything which handicaps you, keeps you back and makes you unhappy. Throw away all useless baggage, drop everything that is a drag, that hinders your progress.

Enter upon tomorrow with a clean slate and a free mind. Don't be mortgaged to the past, and never look back.

There is no use in castigating yourself for not having done better.

Form a habit of expelling from your mind thoughts or suggestions which call up unpleasant subjects or bitter memories, and which have a bad influence upon you.

Every one ought to make it a life rule to wipe out from his memory everything that has been unpleasant, unfortunate. We ought to forget everything that has kept us back, has made us suffer, has been disagreeable, and never allow the hideous pictures of distressing conditions to enter our minds again. There is only one thing to do with a disagreeable, harmful experience, and that is—forget it!

There are many times in the life of a person who does things that are worthwhile when he gets terribly discouraged and thinks it easier to go back than to push on. But there is no victory in retreating. We should never leave any bridges unburned behind us, any way open for retreat to tempt our weakness, indecision or discouragement. If there is anything we ever feel grateful for, it is that we have had courage and pluck enough to push on, to keep going when things looked dark and when seemingly insurmountable obstacles confronted us.

Most people are their own worst enemies. We are all the time "queering" our life game by our vicious, tearing-down thoughts and unfortunate moods. Everything depends upon our courage, our faith in ourselves, in our holding a hopeful, optimistic outlook; and yet, whenever things go wrong with us, whenever we have a discouraging day or an unfortunate experience, a loss or any misfortune, we let the tearing-down thought, doubt, fear, despondency, like a bull in a china shop, tear through our mentalities, perhaps breaking up and destroying the work of years of building up, and we have to start all over again. We work and live like the frog in the well; we climb up only to fall back, and often lose all we gain.

One of the worst things that can ever happen to a person is to get it into his head that he was born unlucky and that the Fates are against him. There are no Fates, outside of our own mentality. We are our own Fates. We control our own destiny.

There is no fate or destiny which puts one man down and another up. "It is not in our stars, but in ourselves, that we are underlings." He only is beaten who admits it. The man is inferior who admits that he is inferior, who voluntarily takes an inferior position because he thinks the best things were intended for somebody else.

You will find that just in proportion as you increase your confidence in yourself by the affirmation of what you wish to be and to do, your ability will increase.

No matter what other people may think about your ability, never allow yourself to doubt that you can do or become what you long to. Increase your self-confidence in every possible way, and you can do this to a remarkable degree by the power of self-suggestion.

This form of suggestion—talking to oneself vigorously, earnestly—seems to arouse the sleeping forces in the subconscious self, more effectually than thinking the same thing.

There is a force in words spoken aloud which is not stirred by going over the same words mentally. They sometimes arouse slumbering energies within us which thinking does not stir up—especially if we have not been trained to think deeply, to focus the mind closely. They make a more lasting impression upon the mind, just as words which pass through the eye from the printed page make a greater impression on the brain than we get by thinking the same words; as seeing objects of nature makes a more lasting impression upon the mind than thinking about them. A vividness, a certain force, accompanies the spoken word— especially if earnestly, vehemently uttered— which is not apparent to many in merely thinking about what the words express. If you repeat a firm resolve to yourself aloud, vigorously, even vehemently, you are more likely to carry it to reality than if you merely resolve in silence.

We become so accustomed to our silent thoughts that the voicing of them, the giving audible expression to our yearnings, makes a much deeper impression upon us.

The audible self-encouragement treatment may be used with marvelous results in correcting our weaknesses; overcoming our deficiencies.

Never allow yourself to think meanly, narrowly, poorly of yourself. Never regard yourself as weak, inefficient, diseased, but as perfect, complete, capable. Never even think of the possibility of going through life a failure or a partial failure. Failure and misery are not for the man who has seen the God side of himself, who has been in touch with divinity. They are for those who have never discovered themselves and their godlike qualities.

Stoutly assert that there is a place for you in the world, and that you are going to fill it like a man. Train yourself to expect great things of yourself. Never admit, even by your manner, that you think you are destined to do little things all your life.

It is marvelous what mental strength can be developed by the perpetual affirmation of vigorous fitness, strength, power, efficiency; these are thoughts and ideals that make a strong man.

The way to get the best out of yourself is to put things right up to yourself, handle yourself without gloves, and talk to yourself as you would to a son of yours who has great ability but who is not using half of it.

When you go into an undertaking just say to yourself, "Now, this thing is right up to me. I've got to make good, to show the man in me or the coward. There is no backing out."

You will be surprised to see how quickly this sort of self-suggestion will brace you up and put new spirit in you.

I have a friend who has helped himself wonderfully by talking to himself about his conduct. When he feels that he is not doing all that he ought to, that he has made some foolish mistake or has failed to use good sense and good judgment in any transaction, when he feels that his stamina and ambition are deteriorating, he goes off alone to the country, to the woods if possible, and has a good heart-to-heart talk with himself something after this fashion:

"Now young man, you need a good talking-to, a bracing-up all along the line. You are going stale, your standards are dropping, your ideals are getting dull, and the worst of it all is that when you do a poor job, or are careless about your dress and indifferent in your manner, you do not feel as troubled as you used to. You are not making good. This lethargy, this inertia, this indifference will seriously cripple your career if you're not very careful. You are letting a lot of good chances slip by you, because you are not as progressive and up-to-date as you ought to be.

"In short, you are becoming lazy. You like to take things easy. Nobody ever amounts to much who lets his energies flag, his standards droop and his ambition ooze out. Now, I am going to keep right after you, young man, until you are doing yourself justice. This take-it-easy sort of policy will never land you at the goal you started for. You will have to watch yourself very closely or you will be left behind.

"You are capable of something much better than what you are doing. You must start out today with a firm resolution to make the returns from your work greater tonight than ever before. You must make this a red-letter day. Bestir yourself; get the cobwebs out of your head; brush off the brain ash. Think, think, think to some purpose! Do not mull and mope like this. You are only half-alive, man; get a move on you!"

This young man says that every morning when he finds his standards are down and he feels lazy and indifferent he "hauls himself over the coals," as he calls it, in order to force himself up to a higher standard and put himself in tune for the day. It is the very first thing he attends to.

He forces himself to do the most disagreeable tasks first, and does not allow himself to skip hard problems. "Now, don't be a coward," he says to himself. "If others have done this, you can do it."

By years of stern discipline of this kind he has done wonders with himself. He began as a poor boy living in the slums of New York with no one to take an interest in him, encourage or push him. Though he had little opportunity for schooling when he was a small boy, he has given himself a splendid education, mainly since he was 21. I have never known anyone else who carried on such a vigorous campaign in self-victory, self-development, self-training, self-culture as this young man has.

At first it may seem silly to you to be talking to yourself, but you will derive so much benefit from it that you will have recourse to it in remedying all your defects. There is no fault, however great or small, which will not succumb to persistent audible suggestion. For example, you may be naturally timid and shrink from meeting people; and you may distrust your own ability. If so, you will be greatly helped by assuring yourself in your daily self-talks that you are not timid; that, on the contrary, you are the embodiment of courage and bravery. Assure yourself that there is no reason why you should be timid, because there is nothing inferior or peculiar about you; that you are attractive and that you know how to act in the presence of others. Say to yourself that you are never again going to allow yourself to harbor any thoughts of self-depreciation or timidity or inferiority; that you are going to hold your head up and go about as though you were a king, a conqueror, instead of crawling about like a whipped cur; you are going to assert your manhood, your individuality.

If you lack initiative, stoutly affirm your ability to begin things, and to push them to a finish. And always put your resolve into action at the first opportunity.

You will be surprised to see how you can increase your courage, your confidence, and your ability, if you will be sincere with yourself and strong and persistent in your affirmations.

I know of nothing so helpful for the timid, those who lack faith in themselves, as the habit of constantly affirming their own importance, their own power, their own divinity. The trouble is that we do not think half enough of ourselves; do not accurately measure our ability; do not put the right estimate upon our possibilities. We berate ourselves, belittle, efface ourselves, because we do not see the larger, diviner man in us.

Try this experiment the very next time you get discouraged or think that you are a failure, that your work does not amount to much— turn about face. Resolve that you will go no further in that direction. Stop and face the other way, and go the other way. Every time you think you are a failure, it helps you to become one, for your thought is your life pattern and you cannot get away from it. You cannot get away from your ideals, the standard which you hold for yourself, and if you acknowledge in your thought that you are a failure, that you can't do anything worthwhile, that luck is against you, that you don't have the same opportunity that other people have—your convictions will control the result.

There are thousands of people who have lost everything they valued in the world, all the material results of their lives' endeavor, and yet, because they possess stout hearts, unconquerable spirits, a determination to push ahead which knows no retreat, they are just as far from real failure as before their loss; and with such wealth they can never be poor.

A great many people fail to reach a success which matches their ability because they are victims of their moods, which repel people and repel business.

We avoid morose, gloomy people just as we avoid a picture which makes a disagreeable impression upon us.

Everywhere we see people with great ambitions doing very

ordinary things, simply because there are so many days when they do not "feel like it" or when they are discouraged or "blue."

A man who is at the mercy of a capricious disposition can never be a leader, a power among men.

It is perfectly possible for a well-trained mind to completely rout the worst case of the "blues" in a few minutes; but the trouble with most of us is that instead of flinging open the mental blinds and letting in the sun of cheerfulness, hope, and optimism, we keep them closed and try to eject the darkness by main force.

The art of arts is learning how to clear the mind of its enemies— enemies of our comfort, happiness, and success. It is a great thing to learn to focus the mind upon the beautiful instead of the ugly, the true instead of the false, upon harmony instead of discord, life instead of death, health instead of disease. This is not always easy, but it is possible to everybody. It requires only skillful thinking, the forming of the right thought habits.

The best way to keep out darkness is to keep the life filled with light; to keep out discord, keep it filled with harmony; to shut out error, keep the mind filled with truth; to shut out ugliness, contemplate beauty and loveliness; to get rid of all that is sour and unwholesome, contemplate all that is sweet and wholesome. Opposite thoughts cannot occupy the mind at the same time.

No matter whether you feel like it or not, just affirm that you must feel like it, that you will feel like it, that you do feel like it, that you are normal and that you are in a position to do your best. Say it deliberately, affirm it vigorously and it will come true.

The next time you get into trouble, or are discouraged and think you are a failure, just try the experiment of affirming vigorously, persistently, that all that is real must be good, for God made all that is, and whatever doesn't seem to be good is not like its creator and therefore cannot be real. Persist in this affirmation. You will be surprised to see how unfortunate suggestions and adverse conditions will melt away before it.

The next time you feel the "blues" or a fit of depression coming on, just get by yourself—if possible after taking a good bath and dressing yourself becomingly—and give yourself a good talking-to.

Talk to yourself in the same dead-in-earnest way that you would talk to your own child or a dear friend who was deep in the mire of despondency, suffering tortures from melancholy. Drive out the black, hideous pictures which haunt your mind. Sweep away all depressing thoughts, suggestions, all the rubbish that is troubling you. Let go of everything that is unpleasant; all the mistakes, all the disagreeable past; just rise up in arms against the enemies of your peace and happiness; summon all the force you can muster and drive them out. Resolve that no matter what happens you are going to be happy; that you are going to enjoy yourself.

When you look at it squarely, it is very foolish—almost criminal— to go about this beautiful world, crowded with splendid opportunities, and things to delight and cheer us, with a sad, dejected face, as though life had been a disappointment instead of a priceless boon. Just say to yourself, "I am a man and I am going to do the work of a man. It's right up to me and I am going to face the situation."

Do not let anybody or anything shake your faith that you can conquer all the enemies of your peace and happiness, and that you inherit an abundance of all that is good.

We should early form the habit of erasing from the mind all disagreeable, unhealthy, death-dealing thoughts. We should start out every morning with a clean slate. We should blot out from our mental gallery all discordant pictures and replace them with the harmonious, uplifting, life-giving ones.

The next time you feel jaded, discouraged, completely played out and "blue," you will probably find, if you look for the reason, that your condition is largely due to exhausted vitality, either from overwork, overeating, or violating in some way the laws of digestion, or from vicious habits of some kind.

The "blues" are often caused by exhausted nerve cells, due to overstraining work, long-continued excitement, or overstimulated nerves from dissipation. This condition is caused by the clamoring of exhausted nerve cells for nourishment, rest, or recreation. Multitudes of people suffer from despondency and melancholy, as a result of a run-down condition physically, due to their irregular, vicious habits, and a lack of refreshing sleep.

When you are feeling "blue" or discouraged, get as complete a change of environment as possible. Whatever you do, do not brood over your troubles or dwell upon the things which happen to annoy you at the time. Think the pleasantest, happiest things possible. Hold the most charitable, loving thoughts toward others. Make a strenuous effort to radiate joy and gladness to everybody about you. Say the kindest, pleasantest things. You will soon begin to feel a wonderful uplift; the shadows which darkened your mind will flee away, and the sun of joy will light up your whole being.

Stoutly, constantly, everlastingly affirm that you will become what your ambitions indicate as fitting and possible. Do not say, "I shall be a success sometime"; say, "I am a success. Success is my birthright." Do not say that you are going to be happy in the future. Say to yourself, "I was intended for happiness, made for it, and I am happy now."

If, however, you affirm, "I am health; I am prosperity; I am this or that," but do not believe it, you will not be helped by affirmation. You must believe what you affirm and try to realize it.

Assert your actual possession of the things you need; of the qualities you long to have. Force your mind toward your goal; hold it there steadily, persistently, for this is the mental state that creates. The negative mind, which doubts and wavers, creates nothing.

"I, myself, am good fortune," says Walt Whitman. If we could only realize that the very attitude of assuming that we are the real embodiment of the thing we long to be or to attain, that we possess the good things we long for, not that we possess all the qualities of good, but that we are these qualities—with the constant affirming, "I myself am good luck, good fortune; I am myself a part of the great creative, sustaining principle of the universe, because my real, divine self and my Father are one"—what a revolution would come to earth's toilers!

Chapter
45

STAND FOR SOMETHING

The greatest thing that can be said of a man, no matter how much he has achieved, is that he has kept his record clean.

Why is it that, in spite of the ravages of time, the reputation of Lincoln grows larger and his character means more to the world every year? It is because he kept his record clean, and never prostituted his ability nor gambled with his reputation.

Where, in all history, is there an example of a man who was merely rich, no matter how great his wealth, who exerted such a power for good, who was such a living force in civilization, as was this poor backwoods boy? What a powerful illustration of the fact that character is the greatest force in the world!

A man assumes importance and becomes a power in the world just as soon as it is found that he stands for something; that he is not for sale; that he will not lease his manhood for salary, for any amount of money or for any influence or position; that he will not lend his name to anything which he cannot endorse.

The trouble with so many men today is that they do not stand for anything outside their vocation. They may be well educated, well up in their specialties, may have a lot of expert knowledge, but they cannot be depended upon. There is some flaw in them which takes the edge off their virtue. They may be fairly honest, but you cannot bank on them.

It is not difficult to find a lawyer or a physician who knows a good deal, who is eminent in his profession; but it is not so easy to find one who is a man before he is a lawyer or a physician; whose name is a synonym for all that is clean, reliable, solid, substantial. It is not difficult to find a good preacher; but it is not so easy to find a real man, sterling manhood, back of the sermon. It is easy to find successful merchants, but not so easy to find men who put character above merchandise. What the world wants is men who have principle underlying their expertness—principle under their law, their medicine, their business; men who stand for something outside of their offices and stores; who stand for something in their community; whose very presence carries weight.

Everywhere we see smart, clever, longheaded, shrewd men, but how comparatively rare it is to find one whose record is as clean as a hound's tooth; who will not swerve from the right; who would rather fail than be a party to a questionable transaction!

Everywhere we see businessmen putting the stumbling blocks of deception and dishonest methods right across their own pathway, tripping themselves up while trying to deceive others.

We see men worth millions of dollars filled with terror; trembling lest investigations may uncover things which will damn them in the public estimation! We see them cowed before the law like whipped spaniels; catching at any straw that will save them from public disgrace!

What a terrible thing to live in the limelight of popular favor, to be envied as rich and powerful, to be esteemed as honorable and straightforward, and yet to be conscious all the time of not being what the world thinks we are; to live in constant terror of discovery, in fear that something may happen to unmask us and show us up in our true light! But nothing can happen to injure seriously the man who lives four-square to the world; who has nothing to cover up, nothing to hide from his fellows; who lives a transparent, clean life, with never a fear of disclosures. If all of his material possessions are swept away from him, he knows that he has a monument in the hearts of his countrymen, in the affection and admiration of the people, and that nothing can happen to harm his real self because he has kept his record clean.

Mr. Roosevelt early resolved that, let what would come, whether he succeeded in what he undertook or failed, whether he made friends or enemies, he would not take chances with his good name—he would part with everything else first; that he would never gamble with his reputation; that he would keep his record clean. His first ambition was to stand for something, to be a man. Before he was a politician or anything else the man must come first.

Theodore Roosevelt

In his early career he had many opportunities to make a great deal of money by allying himself with crooked, sneaking, unscrupulous politicians. He had all sorts of opportunities for political graft. But crookedness never had any attraction for him. He refused to be a party to any political jobbery, any underhand business. He preferred to lose any position he was seeking, to let somebody else have it, if he must get smirched in the getting it. He would not touch a dollar, place, or preferment unless it came to him clean, with no trace of jobbery on it.

Politicians who had an "ax to grind" knew it was no use to try to bribe him, or to influence him with promises of patronage, money, position, or power. Mr. Roosevelt knew perfectly well that he would make many mistakes and many enemies, but he resolved to carry himself in such a way that even his enemies should at least respect him for his honesty of purpose, and for his straightforward, "square-deal" methods. He resolved to keep his record clean, his name white, at all hazards. Everything else seemed unimportant in comparison.

In times like these the world especially needs such men as Mr. Roosevelt—men who hew close to the chalk line of right and hold the line plumb to truth; men who do not pander to public favor; men who make duty and truth their goal and go straight to their mark, turning neither to the right nor to the left, though a paradise tempts them.

Who can ever estimate how much his influence has done toward purging politics and elevating the American ideal. He has changed the viewpoint of many statesmen and politicians. He has shown them a new and a better way. He has made many of them ashamed of the old methods of grafting and selfish greed. He has held up a new ideal, shown them that unselfish service to their country is infinitely nobler than an ambition for self-aggrandizement. American patriotism has a higher meaning today, because of the example of this great American. Many young politicians and statesmen have adopted cleaner methods and higher aims because of his influence. There is no doubt that tens of thousands of young men in this country are cleaner in their lives, and more honest and ambitious to be good citizens, because here is a man who always stands for the "square deal," for civic righteousness, for American manhood.

Every man ought to feel that there is something in him that bribery cannot touch, that influence cannot buy; something that is not for sale; something he would not sacrifice or tamper with for any price; something he would give his life for if necessary.

If a man stands for something worthwhile, compels recognition for himself alone, on account of his real worth, he is not dependent upon recommendations upon fine clothes, a fine house, or a pull. He is his own best recommendation.

The young man who starts out with the resolution to make his character his capital, and to pledge his whole manhood for every obligation he enters into, will not be a failure, though he wins neither fame nor fortune. No man ever really does a great thing who loses his character in the process.

No substitute has ever yet been discovered for honesty. Multitudes of people have gone to the wall trying to find one. Our prisons are full of people who have attempted to substitute something else for it.

No man can really believe in himself when he is occupying a false position and wearing a mask; when the little monitor within him is constantly saying, "You know you are a fraud; you are not the man you pretend to be." The consciousness of not being genuine, not being what others think him to be, robs a man of power, honeycombs the character, and destroys self-respect and self-confidence.

When Lincoln was asked to take the wrong side of a case he said, "I could not do it. All the time while talking to that jury I should be thinking, 'Lincoln, you're a liar, you're a liar,' and I believe I should forget myself and say it out loud."

Character as capital is very much underestimated by a great number of young men. They seem to put more emphasis upon smartness, shrewdness, longheadedness, cunning, influence, a pull, than upon downright honesty and integrity of character. Yet why do scores of concerns pay enormous sums for the use of the name of a man who, perhaps, has been dead for half a century or more? It is because there is power in that name; because there is character in it; because it stands for something; because it represents reliability and square dealing. Think of what the name of Tiffany, of Park and Tilford, or any of the great names which stand in the commercial world as solid and immovable as the rock of Gibraltar, are worth!

Does it not seem strange that young men who know these facts should try to build up a business on a foundation of cunning, scheming, and trickery, instead of building on the solid rock of character, reliability, and manhood? Is it not remarkable that so many men should work so hard to establish a business on an unreliable, flimsy foundation, instead of building upon the solid masonry of honest goods, square dealing, reliability?

A name is worth everything until it is questioned; but when suspicion clings to it, it is worth nothing. There is nothing in this world that will take the place of character. There is no policy in the world, to say nothing of the right or wrong of it, that compares with honesty and square dealing.

In spite of, or because of, all the crookedness and dishonesty that is being uncovered, of all the scoundrels that are being unmasked, integrity is the biggest word in the business world today. There never was a time in all history when it was so big, and it is growing bigger. There never was a time when character meant so much in business; when it stood for so much everywhere as it does today.

There was a time when the man who was the shrewdest and sharpest and cunningest in taking advantage of others got the biggest salary; but today the man at the other end of the bargain is looming up as never before.

Nathan Straus, when asked the secret of the great success of his firm, said it was their treatment of the man at the other end of the bargain. He said they could not afford to make enemies; they could not afford to displease or to take advantage of customers, or to give them reason to think that they had been unfairly dealt with—that, in the long run, the man who gave the squarest deal to the man at the other end of the bargain would get ahead fastest.

There are merchants who have made great fortunes, but who do not carry weight among their fellow men because they have dealt all their lives with inferiority. They have lived with shoddy and shams so long that the suggestion has been held in their minds until their whole standards of life have been lowered; their ideals have shrunken; their characters have partaken of the quality of their business.

Contrast these men with the men who stood for half a century or more at the head of solid houses, substantial institutions; men who have always stood for quality in everything; who have surrounded themselves not only with ability but with men and women of character.

We instinctively believe in character. We admire people who stand for something; who are centered in truth and honesty. It is not necessary that they agree with us. We admire them for their strength, the honesty of their opinions, the inflexibility of their principles.

The late Carl Schurz was a strong man and antagonized many people. He changed his political views very often; but even his worst enemies knew there was one thing he would never go back on, friends or no friends, party or no party—and that was his devotion to principle as he saw it. There was no parleying with his convictions. He could stand alone, if necessary, with all the world against him. His inconsistencies, his many changes in parties and politics, could not destroy the universal admiration for the man who stood for his convictions. Although he escaped from a German prison and fled his country, where he had been arrested on account of his revolutionary principles when but a mere youth, Emperor William the First had such a profound respect for his honesty of purpose and his strength of character that he invited him to return to Germany and visit him, gave him a public dinner, and paid him great tribute.

Who can estimate the influence of President Eliot in enriching and uplifting our national ideas and standards through the thousands of students who go out from Harvard University? The tremendous force and nobility of character of Phillips Brooks raised everyone who came within his influence to higher levels. His great earnestness in trying to lead people up to his lofty ideals swept everything before it. One could not help feeling while listening to him and watching him that there was a mighty triumph of character, a grand expression of superb manhood. Such men as these increase our faith in the race; in the possibilities of the grandeur of the coming man. We are prouder of our country because of such standards.

It is the ideal that determines the direction of the life. And what a grand sight, what an inspiration, are those men who sacrifice the dollar to the ideal!

The principles by which the problem of success is solved are right and justice, honesty and integrity; and just in proportion as a man deviates from these principles, he falls short of solving his problem.

It is true that he may reach something. He may get money, but is that success? The thief gets money, but does he succeed? Is it any honest to steal by means of a long head than by means of a long arm? It is very much more dishonest, because the victim is deceived and then robbed—a double crime.

We often receive letters which read like this:

"I am getting a good salary; but I do not feel right about it, somehow. I cannot still the voice within me that says, 'Wrong, wrong,' to what I am doing."

"Leave it, leave it," we always say to the writers of these letters. "Do not stay in a questionable occupation, no matter what inducement it offers. Its false light will land you on the rocks if you follow it. It is demoralizing to the mental faculties, paralyzing to the character, to do a thing which one's conscience forbids."

Tell the employer who expects you to do questionable things that you cannot work for him unless you can put the trademark of your manhood, the stamp of your integrity, upon everything you do. Tell him that if the highest thing in you cannot bring success, surely the lowest cannot. You cannot afford to sell the best thing in you, your honor, your manhood, to a dishonest man or a lying institution. You should regard even the suggestion that you might sell out for a consideration as an insult.

Resolve that you will not be paid for being something less than a man; that you will not lease your ability, your education, your inventiveness, your self-respect, for salary, to do a man's lying for him; either in writing advertisements, selling goods, or in any other capacity.

Resolve that, whatever your vocation, you are going to stand for something; that you are not going to be merely a lawyer, a physician, a merchant, a clerk, a farmer, a congressman, or a man who carries a big money bag; but that you are going to be a man first, last, and all the time.

Though the mills of God grind slowly,
yet they grind exceeding small;
Though with patience He stands waiting,
with exactness grinds He all.

—Friedrich von Logau

Because sentence against an evil work is not executed
speedily, therefore the heart of the sons of men is
fully set in them to do evil.

—Ecclesiastes 8:11

Man is a watch, wound up at first but never
Wound up again: once down he's down forever.

—Robert Herrick

Old age seizes upon an ill-spent youth like fire upon a
rotten house.

—Robert South

Last Sunday a young man died here of extreme old age
at twenty-five.

—John Newton

If you will not hear Reason, she'll surely rap your knuckles.

—Poor Richard's Sayings

Chapter
46

NATURE'S LITTLE BILL

"Oh! oh! ah!" exclaimed Franklin; "what have I done to merit these cruel sufferings?" "Many things," replied the Gout; "you have eaten and drunk too freely, and too much indulged those legs of yours in your indolence."

Nature seldom presents her bill on the day you violate her laws. But if you overdraw your account at her bank, and give her a mortgage on your body, be sure she will foreclose. She may loan you all you want; but, like Shylock, she will demand the last ounce of flesh. She rarely brings in her cancer bill before the victim is 40 years old. She does not often annoy a man with her drink bill until he is past his prime, and then presents it in the form of Bright's disease, fatty degeneration of the heart, drunkard's liver, or some similar disease. What you pay the saloon keeper is but a small part of your score.

We often hear it said that the age of miracles is past. We marvel that a thief dying on the cross should appear that very day in Paradise; but behold how that bit of meat or vegetable on a Hawarden breakfast table is snatched from Death, transformed into thought, and on the following night shakes Parliament in the magnetism and oratory of a Gladstone. The age of miracles past, when three times a day right before our eyes Nature performs miracles greater even than raising the dead? Watch that crust of bread thrown into a cell in Bedford Jail and devoured by a poor, hungry tinker; cut, crushed, ground, driven by muscles, dissolved by acids and alkalis; absorbed and hurled into the mysterious red river of life. Scores of little factories along this strange stream, waiting for this crust, transmute it as it passes, as if by magic, here into a bone cell, there into gastric juice, here into bile, there into a nerve cell, yonder into a brain cell.

We cannot trace the processes by which this crust arrives at the muscle and acts, arrives at the brain and thinks. We cannot see the manipulating hand which throws back and forth the shuttle which weaves Bunyan's destinies, nor can we trace the subtle alchemy which transforms this prison crust into the finest allegory in the world, the *Pilgrim's Progress*. But we do know that, unless we supply food when the stomach begs and clamors, brain and muscle cannot continue to act; and we also know that unless the food is properly chosen, unless we eat it properly, unless we maintain good digestion by exercise of mind and body, it will not produce the speeches of a Gladstone or the allegories of a Bunyan.

Truly we are fearfully and wonderfully made. Imagine a cistern which would transform the foul sewage of a city into pure drinking water in a second's time, as the black venous blood, foul with the ashes of burned-up brain cells and debris of worn-out tissues, is transformed in the lungs, at every breath, into pure, bright, red blood. Each drop of blood from that magic stream of liquid life was compounded by a divine Chemist. In it float all our success and destiny. In it are the extensions and limits of our possibilities.

In it are health and long life, or disease and premature death. In it are our hopes and our fears, our courage, our cowardice, our energy or lassitude, our strength or weakness, our success or failure. In it are susceptibilities of high or broad culture, or pinched or narrow faculties handed down from an uncultured ancestry. From it our bones and nerves, our muscles and brain, our comeliness or ugliness, all come. In it are locked up the elements of a vicious or a gentle life, the tendencies of a criminal or a saint. How important is it, then, that we should obey the laws of health, and thus maintain the purity and power of this our earthly River of Life!

"We hear a great deal about the 'vile body,'" said Spenser, "and many are encouraged by the phrase to transgress the laws of health. But Nature quietly suppresses those who treat thus disrespectfully one of her highest products, and leaves the world to be peopled by the descendants of those who are not so foolish."

Nature gives to him that hath. She shows him the contents of her vast storehouse, and bids him take all he wants and be welcome. But she will not let him keep for years what he does not use. Use or lose is her motto. Every atom we do not utilize this great economist snatches from us.

If you put your arm in a sling and do not use it, Nature will remove the muscle almost to the bone, and the arm will become useless, but in exact proportion to your efforts to use it again she will gradually restore what she took away. Put your mind in the sling of idleness, or inactivity, and in like manner she will remove your brain, even to imbecility. The blacksmith wants one powerful arm, and she gives it to him, but reduces the other. You can, if you will, send all the energy of your life into someone faculty, but all your other faculties will starve.

A young lady may wear tight corsets if she chooses, but Nature will remove the rose from her cheek and put pallor there. She will replace a clear complexion with muddy hues and sallow spots. She will take away the elastic step, the luster from the eye.

Don't expect to have health for nothing. Nothing in this world worth anything can be had for nothing. Health is the prize of a constant struggle.

Nature passes no act without affixing a penalty for its violation. Whenever she is outraged, she will have her penalty, although it takes a life.

A great surgeon stood before his class to perform a certain operation which the elaborate mechanism and minute knowledge of modern science had only recently made possible. With strong and gentle hand, he did his work successfully so far as his part of the terrible business went; and then he turned to his pupils and said, "Two years ago a safe and simple operation might have cured this disease. Six years ago, a wise way of life might have prevented it. We have done our best as the case now stands, but Nature will have her word to say. She does not always consent to the repeal of her capital sentences." Next day the patient died.

Apart from accidents, we hold our life largely at will. What business have 75,000 physicians in the United States? It is our own fault that even one-tenth of them get a respectable living. What a commentary upon our modern American civilization that 350,000 people in this country die annually from absolutely preventable diseases! Seneca said, "The gods have given us a long life, but we have made it short." Few people know enough to become old. It is a rare thing for a person to die of old age. Only three or four out of a hundred die of anything like old age. But Nature evidently intended, by the wonderful mechanism of the human body, that we should live well up to a century.

Thomas Parr, of England, lived to the age of 152 years. He was married when he was 120 and did not leave off work until he was 130. The great Dr. Harvey examined Parr's body, but found no cause of death except a change of living. Henry Jenkins, of Yorkshire, England, lived to be 169, and would probably have lived longer had not the king brought him to London, where luxuries hastened his death. The court records of England show that he was a witness in a trial 140 years before his death. He swam across a rapid river when he was a centenarian.

There is nothing we are more ignorant of than the physiology and chemistry of the human body. Not one person in a thousand can correctly locate important internal organs or describe their use in the animal economy.

What an insult to the Creator who fashioned them so wonderfully and fearfully in His own image, that the graduates from our high schools and even universities, and young women who "finish their education," become proficient in the languages, in music, in art, and have the culture of travel, but cannot describe or locate the various organs or functions upon which their lives depend! "The time will come," says Frances Willard, "when it will be told as a relic of our primitive barbarism that children were taught the list of prepositions and the names of the rivers of Thibet, but were not taught the wonderful laws on which their own bodily happiness is based, and the humanities by which they could live in peace and goodwill with those about them." Nothing else is so important to man as the study and knowledge of himself, and yet he knows less of himself than he does of the beasts about him.

The human body is the great poem of the Great Author. Not to learn how to read it, to spell out its meaning, to appreciate its beauties, or to attempt to fathom its mysteries, is a disgrace to our civilization.

What a price mortals pay for their ignorance, let a dwarfed, half-developed, one-sided, short-lived nation answer.

"A brilliant intellect in a sickly body is like gold in a spent swimmer's pocket."

Often, from lack of exercise, one side of the brain gradually becomes paralyzed and deteriorates into imbecility. How intimately the functions of the nervous organs are united! The whole man mourns for a felon. The least swelling presses a nerve against a bone and causes one intense agony, and even a Napoleon becomes a child. A corn on the toe, an affection of the kidneys or of the liver, a boil anywhere on the body, or a carbuncle, may seriously affect the eyes and even the brain. The whole system is a network of nerves, of organs, of functions, which are so intimately joined, and related in such close sympathy, that an injury to one part is immediately felt in every other.

Nature takes note of all our transactions, physical, mental, or moral, and places every item promptly to our debit or credit.

Let us take a look at a page in Nature's ledger:

To damage to the heart in youth by immoderate athletics, tobacco chewing, cigarette smoking, drinking strong tea or coffee, rowing, running to trains, overstudy, excitement, etc.	The "irritable heart," the "tobacco heart," a life of promise impaired or blighted.
To one digestive apparatus ruined by eating hurriedly, by eating unsuitable or poorly cooked food, by drinking ice water when one is heated, by swallowing scalding drinks, especially tea, which forms tannic acid on the delicate lining of the stomach, or by eating when tired or worried, or after receiving bad news, when the gastric juice cannot be secreted, etc.	Dyspepsia, melancholia, years of misery to self, anxiety to one's family, pity and disgust of friends.
To one nervous system shattered by dissipation, abuses, overexcitement, a fast life, feverish haste to get riches or fame, hastening puberty by stimulating food, exciting life, etc.	Years of weakness, disappointed ambition, hopeless inefficiency, a burnt-out life.
To damage by undue mental exertion by burning the "midnight oil," exhausting the brain cells faster than they can be renewed.	Impaired powers of mind, softening of the brain, blighted hopes.
To overstraining the brain trying to lead his class in college, trying to take a prize, or to get ahead of somebody else.	A disappointed ambition, a life of invalidism.
To hardening the delicate and sensitive gray matter of the brain and nerves, and ruining the lining membranes of the stomach and nervous system by alcohol, opium, etc.	A hardened brain, a hardened conscience, a ruined home, Bright's disease, fatty degeneration, nervous degeneration, a short, useless, wasted life.
By forced balances, here and there.	Accounts closed. Physiological and moral bankruptcy.

Sometimes two or three such items are charged to a single account. To offset them, there is placed on the credit side a little feverish excitement, too fleeting for calm enjoyment, followed by regret, remorse, and shame. Be sure your sins will find you out. They are all recorded.

The gods are just, and of our pleasant vices
Make instruments to scourge us.

It is a wonder that we live at all. We violate every law of our being, yet we expect to live to a ripe old age. What would you think of a man who, having an elegant watch delicately adjusted to heat and cold, should leave it on the sidewalk with cases open on a dusty or a rainy day, and yet expect it to keep good time? What would you think of a householder who should leave the doors and windows of his mansion open to thieves and tramps, to winds and dust and rain?

What are our bodies but timepieces made by an Infinite Hand, wound up to run a century, and so delicately adjusted to heat and cold that the temperature will not vary half a degree between the heat of summer and the cold of winter whether we live in the regions of eternal frost or under the burning sun of the tropics? A particle of dust or the slightest friction will throw this wonderful timepiece out of order, yet we often leave it exposed to all the corroding elements. We do not always keep open the 25 miles of ventilating pores in the skin by frequent bathing. We seldom lubricate the delicate wheels of the body with the oil of gladness. We expose it to dust and cinders, cold and draughts, and poisonous gases.

How careful we are to filter our water, air our beds, ventilate our sleeping rooms, and analyze our milk! We shrink from contact with filth and disease. But we put paper colored with arsenic on our walls, and daily breathe its poisonous exhalations. We frequent theaters crowded with human beings, many of whom are uncleanly and diseased. We sit for hours and breathe in upon 1,400 square feet of lung tissue the heated, foul, and heavy air; carbonic acid gas from hundreds of gas burners, each consuming as much oxygen as six people; air filled with shreds of tissue expelled from diseased lungs; poisonous effluvia exhaled from the bodies of people who rarely bathe, from clothing seldom washed, fetid breaths, and skin disease in different stages of development. For hours we sit in this bath of poison, and wonder at our headache and lassitude next morning.

We pour a glass of ice water into a stomach busy in the delicate operation of digestion, ignorant or careless of the fact that it takes half an hour to recover from the shock and get the temperature back to 98 degrees, so that the stomach can go on secreting gastric juice. Then down goes another glass of water with similar results.

We pour down alcohol which thickens the velvety lining of the stomach, and hardens the soft tissues, the thin sheaths of nerves, and the gray matter of the brain. We crowd meats, vegetables, pastry, confectionery, nuts, raisins, wines, fruits, etc., into one of the most delicately constructed organs of the body, and expect it to take care of its miscellaneous and incongruous load without a murmur.

After all these abuses we do not give the blood a chance to go to the stomach and help it out of its misery, but summon it to the brain and muscles, notwithstanding the fact that it is so important to have an extra supply to aid digestion that Nature has made the blood vessels of the alimentary canal large enough to contain several times the amount in the entire body.

Who ever saw a horse leave his oats and hay, when hungry, to wash them down with water? The dumb beasts can teach us some valuable lessons in eating and drinking. Nature mixes our gastric juice or pepsin and acids in just the right proportion to digest our food, and keep it at exactly the right temperature. If we dilute it, or lower its temperature by ice water, we diminish its solvent or digestive power, and dyspepsia is the natural result.

English factory children have received the commiseration of the world because they were scourged to work 14 out of 24 hours. But there is many a theoretical republican who is a harsher taskmaster to his stomach than this; who allows it no more resting time than he does his watch; who gives it no Sunday, no holiday, no vacation in any sense, and who seeks to make his heart beat faster for the sake of the exhilaration he can thus produce.

Although the heart weighs a little over half a pound, yet it pumps 18 pounds of blood from itself, forcing it into every nook and corner of the entire body, back to itself in less than two minutes. This little organ, the most perfect engine in the world, does a daily work equal to lifting 124 tons one foot high, and exerts one-third as much muscle power as does a stout man at hard labor. If the heart should expend its entire force lifting its own weight, it would raise itself nearly 20,000 feet an hour, 10 times as high as a pedestrian can lift himself in ascending a mountain. What folly, then, to goad this willing, hardworking slave to greater exertions by stimulants!

We must pay the penalty of our vocations. Beware of work that kills the workman. Those who prize long life should avoid all occupations which compel them to breathe impure air or deleterious gases, and especially those in which they are obliged to inhale dust and filings from steel and brass and iron, the dust in coal mines, and dust from threshing machines. Stonecutters, miners, and steel grinders are short lived, the sharp particles of dust irritating and inflaming the tender lining of the lung cells. The knife and fork grinders in Manchester, England, rarely live beyond 32 years. Those who work in grain elevators and those who are compelled to breathe chemical poisons are short lived.

Deep breathing in dusty places sends the particles of dust into the upper and less used lobes of the lungs, and these become a constant irritant, until they finally excite an inflammation, which may end in consumption. All occupations in which arsenic is used shorten life.

Dr. William Ogle, who is authority upon this subject, says, "Of all the various influences that tend to produce differences of mortality in any community, none is more potent than the character of the prevailing occupations." Finding that clergymen and priests have the lowest death rate, he represented it as 100, and by comparison found that the rate for inn and hotel servants was 397; miners, 331; earthenware makers, 317; file makers, 300; innkeepers, 274; gardeners, farmers, and agricultural laborers closely approximating the clerical standard. He gave as the causes of high mortality, first, working in a cramped or constrained attitude; second, exposure to the action of poisonous or irritating substances; third, excessive work, mental or physical; fourth, working in confined or foul air; fifth, the use of strong drink; sixth, differences in liability to fatal accidents; seventh, exposure to the inhalation of dust. The deaths of those engaged in alcoholic industries were as 1,521 to 1,000 of the average of all trades.

It is very important that occupations should be congenial. Whenever our work galls us, whenever we feel it to be a drudgery and uncongenial, the friction grinds life away at a terrible rate.

Health can be accumulated, invested, and made to yield its compound interest, and thus be doubled and redoubled. The capital of health may, indeed, be forfeited by one misdemeanor, as a rich man may sink all his property in one bad speculation; but it is as capable of being increased as any other kind of capital.

One is inclined to think with a recent writer that it looks as if the rich men kept out of the kingdom of heaven were also excluded from the kingdom of brains. In New York, Boston, Philadelphia, and Chicago are thousands of millionaires, some of them running through three or four generations of fortune; and yet, in all their ranks, there is seldom a man possessed of the higher intellectual qualities that flower in literature, eloquence, or statesmanship. Scarcely one of them has produced a book worth printing, a poem worth reading, or a speech worth listening to. They are struck with intellectual sterility. They go to college; they travel abroad; they hire the dearest masters; they keep libraries among their furniture; and some of them buy works of art. But, for all that, their brains wither under luxury, often by their own vices or tomfooleries, and mental barrenness is the result. He who violates Nature's law must suffer the penalty, though he has millions. The fruits of intellect do not grow among the indolent rich. They are usually out of the republic of brains. Work or starve is Nature's motto; starve mentally, starve morally, even if you are rich enough to prevent physical starvation.

How heavy a bill Nature collects of him in whom the sexual instinct has been permitted to taint the whole life with illicit thoughts and deeds, stultifying the intellect, deadening the sensibilities, dwarfing the soul!

> *I waive the quantum of the sin,*
> *The hazard of concealing;*
> *But och, it hardens all within,*
> *And petrifies the feeling.*

The sense of fatigue is one of Nature's many signals of danger. All we accomplish by stimulating or crowding the body or mind when tired is worse than lost. Insomnia, and sometimes even insanity, is Nature's penalty for prolonged loss of sleep.

One of the worst tortures of the Inquisition was that of keeping victims from sleeping, often driving them to insanity or death. Melancholy follows insomnia; insanity, both. To keep us in a healthy condition, Nature takes us back to herself, puts us under the ether of sleep, and keeps us there nearly one-third of our lives, while she overhauls and repairs in secret our wonderful mechanism. She takes us back each night wasted and dusty from the day's work, broken, scarred, and injured in the great struggle of life. Each cell of the brain is reburnished and refreshened; all the ashes or waste from the combustion of the tissues is washed out into the blood stream, pumped to the lungs, and thrown out in the breath; and the body is returned in the morning as fresh and good as new. The American honey does not always pay for the sting.

Labor is the eternal condition on which the rich man gains an appetite for his dinner, and the poor man a dinner for his appetite; but the habit of constant, perpetual industry often becomes a disease.

In the Norse legend, Odin was not allowed to drink from Mirmir's Spring, the fount of wisdom, until he had left his eye as a pledge. Scholars often leave their health, their happiness, their usefulness behind, in their great eagerness to drink deep draughts at wisdom's fountain. Professional men often sacrifice everything that is valuable in life for the sake of reputation, influence, and money. Business men sacrifice home, family, health, happiness, in the great struggle for money and power. The American prize, like the pearl in the oyster, is very attractive, but is too often the result of disease.

Charles Linnaeus, the great naturalist, so exhausted his brain by overexertion that he could not recognize his own work, and even forgot his own name. Kirk White won the prize at Cambridge, but it cost him his life. He studied at night and forced his brain by stimulants and narcotics in his endeavor to pull through, but he died at 24. Paley died at 62 of overwork. He was called "one of the sublimest spirits in the world."

President Timothy Dwight of Yale College nearly killed himself by overwork when a young man. When at Yale he studied nine hours, taught six hours a day, and took no exercise whatever. He could not be induced to stop until he became so nervous and irritable that he was unable to look at a book 10 minutes a day. His mind gave way, and it was a long time before he fully recovered.

Imagine the surprise of the angels at the death of men and women in the early prime and vigor of life. Could we but read the notes of their autopsies we might say less of mysterious Providence at funerals. They would run somewhat as follows:

NOTES FROM THE ANGELS' AUTOPSIES

What, is it returned so soon? —a body framed for a century's use returned at 30? —a temple which was 28 years in building destroyed almost before it was completed? What has gray hairs, wrinkles, a bent form, and death to do with youth?Has all this beauty perished like a bud just bursting into bloom, plucked by the grim destroyer? Has she fallen a victim to tight lacing, overexcitement, and the gaiety and frivolity of fashionable life?

Here is an educated, refined woman who died of lung starvation. What a tax human beings pay for breathing impure air! Nature provides them with a tonic atmosphere, compounded by the divine Chemist, but they refuse to breathe it in its purity, and so must pay the penalty in shortened lives. They can live a long time without water, a longer time without food, clothing, or the so-called comfortsof life; they can live without education or culture, but their lungs must have good, healthful air food 24,000 times a day if they would maintain health. Oh, that they would see, as we do, the intimate connection between bad air, bad morals, and a tendency to crime!

Here are the ruins of an idolized son and loving husband. Educated and refined, what infinite possibilities beckoned him onward at the beginning of his career! But the Devil's agent offered him imagination, sprightliness, wit, eloquence, bodily strength, and happiness in eau de vie, or "water of life," as he called it, at only 15 cents a glass. The best of our company tried to dissuade him, but to no avail. The poor mortal closed his "bargain" with the dramseller, and what did he get? A hardened conscience, a ruined home, a diseased body, a muddled brain, a heartbroken wife, wretched children, disappointed friends, triumphant enemies, days of remorse, nights of anguish, an unwept deathbed, an unhonored grave. And only to think that he is only one of many thousands! "What fools these mortals be!"

Did he not see the destruction toward which he was rushing with all the feverish haste of slavish appetite? Ah, yes, but only when it was too late. In his clenched hand, as he lay dead, was found a crumpled paper containing the following, in lines barely legible so tremulous were the nerves of the writer: "Wife, children, and over 40,000 dollars all gone! I alone am responsible. All has gone down my throat. When I was 21, I had a fortune. I am not yet 35 years old. I have killed my beautiful wife, who died of a broken heart; have murdered our children with neglect. When this coin is gone I do not know how I can get my next meal. I shall die a drunken pauper. This is my last money, and my history. If this bill comes into the hands of any man who drinks, let him take warning from my life's ruin."

What a magnificent specimen of manhood this would have been if his life had been under the rule of reason, not passion! He dies of old age at 40, his hair is gray, his eyes are sunken, his complexion sodden, his body marked with the labels of his disease. A physique fit for a god, fashioned in the Creator's image, with infinite possibilities, a physiological hulk wrecked on passion's seas, and fit only for a danger signal to warn the race. What would parents think of a captain who would leave his son in charge of a ship without giving him any instructions or chart showing the rocks, reefs, and shoals? Do they not know that those who sleep in the ocean are but a handful compared with those who have foundered on passion's seas?

Oh, the sins of silence which parents commit against those dearer to them than life itself! Youth cannot understand the great solicitude of parents regarding their education, their associations, their welfare generally, and the mysterious silence in regard to their physical natures. An intelligent explanation, by all mothers to the daughters and by all fathers to the sons, of the mysteries of their physical lives, when at the right age, would revolutionize civilization. This young clergyman killed himself trying to be popular. This student committed suicide by exhausting his brain in trying to lead his class. This young lawyer overdrew his account at Nature's bank, and she foreclosed by a stroke of paralysis. This merchant died at 35 by his own hand. His life was slipping away without enjoyment. He had murdered his capacity for happiness, and dug his own spiritual grave while making preparations for enjoying life. This young society man died of nothing to do and dissipation, at 30.

What a miserable farce the life of men and women seems

to us! *Time, which is so precious that even the Creator will not give a second moment until the first is gone, they throw away as though it were water. Opportunities which angels covet they fling away as of no consequence, and die failures, because they have "no chance in life." Life, which seems so precious to us, they spurn as if but a bauble. Scarcely a mortal returns to us who has not robbed himself of years of precious life. Scarcely a man returns to us dropping off in genuine old age, as autumn leaves drop in the forest.*

Has life become so cheap that mortals thus throw it away?

Habit, if wisely and skillfully formed, becomes truly a second nature.

—*Francis Bacon*

Habit, with its iron sinews, Clasps and leads us day by day.

—*Alphonse de Lamartine*

The chain of habit coils itself around the heart like a serpent, to gnaw and stifle it.

—*William Hazlitt*

You cannot, in any given case, by any sudden and single effort, will to be true, if the habit of your life has been insincerity.

—*F.W. Robertson*

It is a beautiful provision in the mental and moral arrangement of our nature, that that which is performed as a duty may by frequent repetition, become a habit; and the habit of stern virtue, so repulsive to others, may hang around our neck like a wreath of flowers.

—*Paxton Hood*

Chapter
47

HABIT: THE SERVANT—
THE MASTER

"When shall I begin to train my child?" asked a young mother of a learned physician.

"How old is the child?" inquired the doctor. "Two years, sir."

"Then you have lost just two years," replied he, gravely.

"You must begin with his grandmother," said Oliver Wendell Holmes, when asked a similar question.

"At the mouth of the Mississippi," says Beecher, "how impossible would it be to stay its waters, and to separate from each other the drops from the various streams that have poured in on either side—of the Red River, the Arkansas, the Ohio, and the Missouri—or to sift, grain by grain the particles of sand that have been washed from the Alleghany, or the Rocky Mountains; yet how much more impossible would it be when character is the river, and habits are the sidestreams!"

"We sow an act, we reap a habit; we sow a habit, we reap a character."

While correct habits depend largely on self-discipline, and often on self-denial, bad habits, like weeds, spring up, unaided and untrained, to choke the plants of virtue and as with Canada thistles, allowed to go to seed in a fair meadow, we may have "one day's seeding, ten years' weeding."

We seldom see much change in people after they get to be 25 or 30 years of age, except in going further in the way they have started;

but it is a great comfort to think that, when one is young, it is almost as easy to acquire a good habit as a bad one, and that it is possible to be hardened in goodness as well as in evil.

Take good care of the first 20 years of your life, and you may hope that the last 20 will take good care of you.

A writer on the history of Staffordshire tells of an idiot who, living near a town clock, and always amusing himself by counting the hour of the day whenever the clock struck, continued to strike and count the hour correctly without its aid, when at one time it happened to be injured by an accident.

Dr. Johnson had acquired the habit of touching every post he passed in the street; and, if he missed one, he was uneasy, irritable, and nervous till he went back and touched the neglected post.

"Even thought is but a habit."

Heredity is a man's habit transmitted to his offspring.

A special study of hereditary drunkenness has been made by Professor Pellman of Bonn University, Germany. He thus traced the careers of children, grandchildren, and great-grandchildren in all parts of the present German Empire, until he was able to present tabulated biographies of the hundreds descended from some original drunkard.

Notable among the persons described by Professor Pellman is *Frau Ada Jurke*, who was born in 1740, and was a drunkard, a thief, and a tramp for the last 40 years of her life, which ended in 1800. Her descendants numbered 834, of whom 709 were traced in local records from youth to death. One hundred and six of the 709 were born out of wedlock. There were 144 beggars, and 62 more who lived from charity. Of the women, 181 led disreputable lives. There were in the family 76 convicts, 7 of whom were sentenced for murder. In a period of some 75 years, this one family rolled up a bill of costs in almshouses, prisons, and correctional institutions amounting to at least 5,000,000 marks, or about $1,250,000.

Isaac Watts had a habit of rhyming. His father grew weary of it, and set out to punish him, which made the boy cry out:

Pray, father, on me mercy take,
And I will no more verses make.

A minister had a bad habit of exaggeration, which seriously impaired his usefulness. His brethren came to expostulate. With extreme humiliation over this fault as they set it forth, he said, "Brethren, I have long mourned over this fault, and I have shed *barrels of tears* because of it." They gave him up as incorrigible.

Men carelessly or playfully get into habits of speech or act which become so natural that they speak or act as they do not intend, to their discomfiture. Professor Phelps told of some Andover students, who, for sport, interchanged the initial consonants of adjacent words. "But," said he, "retribution overtook them. On a certain morning, when one of them was leading the devotions, he prayed the Lord to 'have mercy on us, feak and weeble sinners.'" The habit had come to possess him.

Many speakers have undesirable habits of utterance or gesture. Some are continually applying the hand to some part of the face, the chin, the whiskers; some give the nose a peck with thumb and forefinger; others have the habit characterized as,

> *Washing the hands with invisible soap*
> *In a bowl of invisible water.*

"We are continually denying that we have habits which we have been practicing all our lives," says Beecher. "Here is a man who has lived 40 or 50 years; and a chance shot sentence or word lances him and reveals to him a trait which he has always possessed, but which, until now, he had not the remotest idea that he possessed. For 40 or 50 years he has been fooling himself about a matter as plain as the nose on his face."

Had the angels been consulted, whether to create man, with this principle introduced, that, if a man did a thing once, if would be easier the second time, and at length would be done without effort, they would have said, "Create!"

Remember that habit is an arrangement, a principle of human nature, which we must use to increase the efficiency and ease of our work in life.

"Make sobriety a habit, and intemperance will be hateful; make prudence a habit, and reckless profligacy will be as contrary to the course of nature in the child, or in the adult, as the most atrocious crimes are to any of us."

Out of hundreds of replies from successful men as to the probable cause of failure, "bad habits" was in almost everyone.

How easy it is to be nobody; it is the simplest thing in the world to drift down the stream, into bad company, into the saloon; just a little beer, just a little gambling, just a little bad company, just a little killing of time, and the work is done.

New Orleans is from 5 to 15 feet below high water in the Mississippi River. The only protection to the city from the river is the levee. In May, 1883, a small break was observed in the levee, and the water was running through. A few bags of sand or loads of dirt would have stopped the water at first; but it was neglected for a few hours, and the current became so strong that all efforts to stop it were fruitless. A reward of 500,000 dollars was offered to any man who would stop it; but it was too late—it could not be done.

Beware of "small sins" and "white lies."

There are four good habits— punctuality, accuracy, steadiness, and dispatch. Without the first, time is wasted; without the second, mistakes the most hurtful to our own credit and interest, and those of others, may be committed; without the third, nothing can be well done; and without the fourth, opportunities of great advantage are lost, which it is impossible to recall."

Abraham Lincoln gained his clear precision of statement of propositions by practice, and Wendell Phillips his wonderful English diction by always thinking and conversing in excellent style.

"Family customs exercise a vast influence over the world. Children go forth from the parents' nest, spreading the habits they have imbibed over every phase of society. These can easily be traced to their sources."

"To be sure, this is only a trifle in itself; but, then, the manner in which I do every trifling thing is of very great consequence, because it is just in these little things that I am forming my business habits. I must see to it that I do not fail here, even if this is only a small task."

"A physical habit is like a tree grown crooked. You cannot go to the orchard, and take hold of a tree grown thus, and straighten it, and say, 'Now keep straight!' and have it obey you. What can you do? You can drive down a stake, and bind the tree to it, bending it back a little, and scarifying the bark on one side. And if, after that, you bend it back a little more every month, keeping it taut through the season, and from season to season, at length you will succeed in making it permanently straight. You can straighten it, but you cannot do it immediately; you must take one or two years for it."

Sir George Staunton visited a man in India who had committed murder; and in order not only to save his life, but what was of much greater consequence to him, his caste, he had submitted to a terrible penalty—to sleep for seven years on a bed, the entire top of which was studded with iron points, as sharp as they could be without penetrating the flesh. Sir George saw him during the fifth year of his sentence. His skin then was like the hide of a rhinoceros; and he could sleep comfortably on his bed of thorns, and he said that at the end of the seven years he thought he should use the same bed from choice. What a vivid parable of a sinful life! Sin, at first a bed of thorns, after a time becomes comfortable through the deadening of moral sensibility.

When the suspension bridge over Niagara River was to be erected, the question was, how to get the cable over. With a favoring wind a kite was elevated, which alighted on the opposite shores. To its insignificant string a cord was attached, which was drawn over, then a rope, then a larger one, then a cable; finally, the great bridge was completed, connecting the United States with Canada.

> *First across the gulf we cast*
> *Kiteborne threads till lines are passed,*
> *And habit builds the bridge at last.*

"Launch your bark on the Niagara River," said John B. Gough; "it is bright, smooth, and beautiful, Down the stream you glide on your pleasure excursion. Suddenly someone cries out from the bank, 'Young men, ahoy!' 'What is it?'

"'The rapids are below you.' 'Ha! ha! we have heard of the rapids, but we are not such fools as to get there. If we go too fast, then we shall up with the helm, and steer to the shore. Then on, boys, don't be alarmed—there is no danger.'

"'Young men, ahoy there!' 'What is it?' 'The rapids are below you!' 'Ha! ha! we will laugh and quaff. What care we for the future? No man ever saw it. Sufficient for the day is the evil thereof. We will enjoy life while we may, will catch pleasure as it flies. There's time enough to steer out of danger.'

"'Young men, ahoy!' 'What is it?' 'Beware! Beware! The rapids are below you!'

"Now you see the water foaming all around. See how fast you pass that point! Up with the helm! Now turn! Pull hard! Quick, quick! Pull for your lives! Pull till the blood starts from the nostrils, and the veins stand like whipcords upon the brow! Set the mast in the socket! hoist the sail—ah! ah! it is too late! Shrieking, cursing, howling, blaspheming, over you go.

"Thousands go over the rapids every year, through the power of habit, crying all the while, 'When I find out that it is injuring me, I will give it up!'"

A community is often surprised and shocked at some crime. The man was seen on the street yesterday, or in his store, but he showed no indication that he would commit such crime today. Yet the crime committed today is but a regular and natural sequence of what the man did yesterday and the day before. It was but a result of the fearful momentum of all his past habits.

A painter once wanted a picture of innocence, and drew from life the likeness of a child at prayer. The little suppliant was kneeling by his mother. The palms of his hands were reverently pressed together, and his mild blue eyes were upturned with the expression of devotion and peace. The portrait was much prized by the painter, who hung it up on his wall, and called it *Innocence*. Years passed away, and the artist became an old man. Still the picture hung there. He had often thought of painting a counterpart—the picture of guilt—but had not found the opportunity. At last, he effected his purpose by paying a visit to a neighboring jail. On the damp floor of his cell lay a wretched culprit heavily ironed. Wasted was his body, and hollow his eyes; vice was visible in his face. The painter succeeded admirably; and the portraits were hung side by side for *Innocence* and *Guilt*. The two originals of the pictures were discovered to be one and the same person—first, in the innocence of childhood! second, in the degradation of guilt and sin and evil habits.

Willpower can be so educated that it will focus the thought upon the bright side of things, upon objects which lift and elevate. Habits of contentment and goodness may be formed the same as any others.

Walking upon the quarterdeck of a vessel, though at first intolerably confining, becomes by custom so agreeable to a sailor that on shore he often hems himself within the same bounds.

Lord Kames tells of a man who, having relinquished the sea for a country life, reared an artificial mount, with a level summit, resembling a quarterdeck not only in shape, but in size, where he generally walked. When Franklin was superintending the erection of some forts on the frontier, as a defense against the Indians, he slept at night in a blanket on a hard floor; and, on his first return to civilized life, he could hardly sleep in a bed. Captain Ross and his crew, having been accustomed, during their polar wanderings, to lie on the frozen snow or a bare rock, afterwards found the accommodations of a whaler too luxurious for them, and the captain exchanged his hammock for a chair.

Two sailors, who had been drinking, took a boat off to their ship. They rowed but made no progress; and presently each began to accuse the other of not working hard enough. Lustily they plied the oars, but after another hour's work still found themselves no farther advanced. By this time, they had become tolerably sober; and one of them, looking over the side, said to the other, "Why, Tom, we haven't pulled the anchor up yet." And thus, it is with those who are anchored to something of which they are not conscious, perhaps, but which impedes their efforts, even though they do their very best.

"A youth thoughtless, when all the happiness of his home forever depends on the chances or the passions of an hour!" exclaims Ruskin. "A youth thoughtless, when his every act is a foundation stone of future conduct, and every imagination a fountain of life or death! Be thoughtless in any after years, rather than now—though, indeed, there is only one place where a man may be nobly thoughtless—his deathbed. No thinking should ever be left to be done there."

Sir James Paget tells us that a practiced musician can play on the piano at the rate of 24 notes a second. For each note a nerve current must be transmitted from the brain to the fingers, and from the fingers to the brain. Each note requires three movements of a finger, the bending down and raising up, and at least one lateral, making no less than 72 motions in a second, each requiring a distinct effort of the will, and directed unerringly with a certain speed, and a certain force, to a certain place.

Some can do this easily, and be at the same time busily employed in intelligent conversation. Thus, by obeying the law of habit until repetition has formed a second nature, we are able to pass the technique of life almost wholly over to the nerve centers, leaving our minds free to act or enjoy.

All through our lives the brain is constantly educating different parts of the body to form habits which will work automatically from reflex action, and thus is delegated to the nervous system a large part of life's duties. This is nature's wonderful economy to release the brain from the drudgery of individual acts, and leave it free to command all its forces for higher service.

Man's lifework is a masterpiece or a botch, according as each little habit has been perfectly or carelessly formed.

It is said that if you invite one of the devil's children to your home the whole family will follow. So, one bad habit seems to have a relationship with all the others. For instance, the one habit of negligence, slovenliness, makes it easier to form others equally bad, until the entire character is honeycombed by the invasion of a family of bad habits.

A man is often shocked when he suddenly discovers that he is considered a liar. He never dreamed of forming such a habit; but the little misrepresentations to gain some temporary end, had, before he was aware of it, made a beaten track in the nerve and brain tissue, until lying has become almost a physical necessity. He thinks he can easily overcome this habit, but he will not. He is bound to it with cords of steel; and only by painful, watchful, and careful repetition of the exact truth, with a special effort of the willpower at each act, can he form a counter trunkline in the nerve and brain tissue.

Society is often shocked by the criminal act of a man who has always been considered upright and true. But, if they could examine the habit map in his nervous mechanism and brain, they would find the beginnings of a path leading directly to his deed, in the tiny repetitions of what he regarded as trivial acts. All expert and technical education is built upon the theory that these trunklines of habit become more and more sensitive to their accustomed stimuli and respond more and more readily.

We are apt to overlook the physical basis of habit. Every repetition of an act makes us more likely to perform that act, and discovers in our wonderful mechanism a tendency to perpetual repetition, whose facility increases in exact proportion to the repetition. Finally, the original act becomes voluntary from a natural reaction.

It is cruel to teach the vicious that they can, by mere force of willpower, turn "about face," and go in the other direction, without explaining to them the scientific process of character building, through habit formation. What we do today is practically what we did yesterday; and, in spite of resolutions, unless carried out in this scientific way, we shall repeat tomorrow what we have done today. How unfortunate that the science of habit forming is not known by mothers, and taught in our schools, colleges, and universities! It is a science compared with which other departments of education sink into insignificance.

The converted man is not always told that the great battle is yet before him; that he must persistently, painfully, prayerfully, and with all the willpower he possesses, break up the old habits, and lay counter lines which will lead to the temple of virtue. He is not told that, in spite of all his efforts, in some unguarded moment, some old switch may be left open, some old desire may flash along the line, and that, possibly before he is aware of it, he may find himself yielding to the old temptation which he had supposed to be conquered forever.

An old soldier was walking home with a beefsteak in one hand and a basket of eggs in the other, when someone yelled, "Halt! Attention!" Instantly the veteran came to a stand; and, as his arms took the position of "attention," eggs and meat went tumbling into the street, the accustomed nerves responding involuntarily to the old stimulus.

Paul evidently understood the force of habit when he declares: *"I find, then, a law, that, when I would do good, evil is present in me. For I delight in the law of God after the inward man: But I see another law in my members, warring against the law in my mind, and bringing me into captivity to the law of sin which is in my members. O wretched man that I am! who shall deliver me from the body of this death!"* (Romans 7:21–24) He referred to the ancient custom of binding a murderer face to face with the dead body of his victim, until suffocated by its stench and dissolution.

"I would give a world, if I had it," said an unfortunate wretch, "to be a true man; yet in 24 hours I may be overcome and disgraced with a shilling's worth of sin."

How shall I a habit break?

As you did that habit make.

As you gathered, you must lose;

As you yielded, now refuse.

Thread by thread the strands we twist,

Till they bind us, neck and wrist;

Thread by thread the patient hand

Must untwine, ere free we stand;

As we builded, stone by stone,

We must toil unhelped, alone,

Till the wall is overthrown.

Chapter
48

THE CIGARETTE

We are so accustomed to the sight and smell of tobacco that we entirely overlook the fact that the tobacco of commerce in all its forms is the product of a poisonous weed. It is first a narcotic and then an irritant poison. It has its place in all toxicological classifications together with its proper antidotes.

Tobacco has not achieved its almost universal popularity without strong opposition. In England, King James launched his famous *Counterblaste* against its use. In Turkey, where men and women are alike slaves to its fascination, tobacco was originally forbidden under severe penalties; the loss of the ears, the slitting of the nostrils and even death itself being penalties imposed for the infraction of the law forbidding the use of tobacco in any form. Since then pipes, cigars, snuff and chewing tobacco have become popularized and tobacco in some form or another is used by almost every nation. The last development in the form of tobacco using was the cigarette rolled between the fingers, and the worst form of the cigarette is the manufactured article sold in cheap packages and freely used by boys who in many cases have not reached their teens.

The manufactured American cigarette seems to be especially deadly in its effect. It is said to contain five and one-half percent of nicotine, or more than twice as much as the Cuban-made cigarette contains, and more than six times as much as is contained in the Turkish cigarette.

I am not going to quarrel with the use of tobacco in general by mature men. He who has come to man's estate is free to decide for himself whether he shall force a poison on his revolting stomach;

for the nausea that follows the first use of tobacco is the stomach's attempt to eject the poison which has been absorbed from pipe, cigar, or cigarette. The grown man, too, is able to determine whether he wants to pay the tax which the use of tobacco levies upon his time, his health, his income and his prosperity. The most that can be said of the use of tobacco is that if habitual users of the narcotic weed are successful in life, they must be successful in spite of the use of tobacco and not because of it; for it is opposed to both reason and common sense that the habitual use of a poison in any form should promote the development and exercise of the faculties whose energetic use is essential to success.

What I desire to do is to warn the boy, the growing youth, of the baneful influence of the cigarette on minds yet unformed, on bodies yet in process of development.

The danger of the cigarette to the growing boy lies first in the fact that it poisons the body. That it does not kill at the outset is due to the fact that the dose is small and so slowly increased that the body gradually accommodates itself to this poison as it does to strychnine, arsenic, opium, and other poisons. But all the time there is a slow but steady process of physical degeneration. The digestion is affected, the heart is overtaxed, liver and bowels are deranged in their functions, and as the poison spreads throughout the system there is a gradual physical deterioration which is marked alike in the countenance and in the carriage of the body. Any person who cares to do so may prove for himself the poisonous nature of nicotine which is derived from tobacco and taken into the system by those who chew or smoke.

Dr. J. J. Kellogg says: "A few months ago I had all the nicotine removed from a cigarette, making a solution of it. I injected half the quantity into a frog, with the effect that the frog died almost instantly. The rest was administered to another frog with like effect. Both frogs were full grown, and of average size. The conclusion is evident that a single cigarette contains poison enough to kill two frogs. A boy who smokes 20 cigarettes a day has inhaled enough poison to kill 40 frogs. Why does the poison not kill the boy? It does tend to kill him. If not immediately, he is likely to die sooner or later of weak heart, Bright's disease, or some other malady which scientific physicians everywhere now recognize as a natural result of chronic nicotine poisoning."

A chemist, not long since, took the tobacco used in an average cigarette and soaked it in several teaspoonfuls of water and then injected a portion of it under the skin of a cat. The cat almost immediately went into convulsions and died in 15 minutes. Dogs have been killed with a single drop of nicotine.

A single drop of nicotine taken from a seasoned pipe, and applied to the tongue of a venomous snake has caused almost instant death.

A Western farmer tried to rear a brood of motherless chickens in his greenhouse. But the chickens did not thrive. They refused to eat; their skins became dry and harsh; their feathers were ruffled; they were feverish and drank constantly. Soon they began to die. As the temperature and general condition of the greenhouse seemed to be especially favorable to the rearing of chickens, the florist was puzzled to determine the cause of their sickness and death. After a careful study of the symptoms, he found that the source of the trouble arose from the fumes of the tobacco stems burned in the greenhouse to destroy green flies and destructive plant parasites.

Though the chickens had always been removed from the greenhouse during the tobacco fumigation and were not returned while any trace of smoke was apparent to the human senses, it was evident that the soil, air, and leaves of the plants retained enough of the poison to keep the chickens in a condition of semi-intoxication. The conditions were promptly changed, and the chickens removed to other quarters recovered rapidly and in a short time were healthy and lively though they were stunted in growth because of this temporary exposure to the effects of nicotine. The symptoms in the chickens were almost identical with the symptoms of nicotine poisoning in young boys, and the effects were relatively the same.

The most moderate use of the cigarette is injurious to the body and mind of the youth; excessive indulgence leads inevitably to insanity and death.

A young man died in a Minnesota state institution not long ago, who, five years before, had been one of the most promising young physicians of the West. "Still under 30 years at the time of his commitment to the institution," says the newspaper account of his story, "he had already made three discoveries in nervous diseases that had made him looked up to in his profession. But he smoked cigarettes—smoked incessantly. For a long time, the effects of the habit were not apparent on him. In fact, it was not until a patient died on the operating table under his hands, and the young doctor went to pieces, that it became known that he was a victim of the paper pipes. But then he had gone too far. He was a wreck in mind as well as in body, and he ended his days in a maniac's cell."

Another unfortunate victim of the cigarette was, not long ago, taken to the Brooklyn Hospital. He was a fireman on the railroad and was only 21 years old. He said he began smoking cigarettes when a mere boy. Before being taken to the hospital he smoked all night for weeks without sleep. When in the hospital he recognized none, but called loudly to everyone he saw to kill him. He would batter his head against the wall in the attempt to commit suicide. At length he was taken to the King's County Hospital in a strait jacket, where death soon relieved him of his sufferings.

Similar results are following the excessive use of cigarettes, every day and in all sections of the country.

"Died of heart failure" is the daily verdict on scores of those who drop down at the desk or in the street. Cannot this sudden taking off, of apparently hale and sturdy men be related, oftentimes to the heart weakness caused by the excessive use of tobacco and particularly of cigarettes?

Excessive cigarette smoking increases the heart's action very materially, in some instances 25 or 30 beats a minute. Think of the enormous amount of extra work forced upon this delicate organ every 24 hours! The pulsations are not only greatly increased but also very materially weakened, so that the blood is not forced to every part of the system, and hence the tissues are not nourished as they would be by means of fewer but stronger, more vigorous pulsations.

The indulgence in cigarettes stunts the growth and retards physical development. An investigation of all the students who entered Yale University during nine years shows that the cigarette smokers were the inferiors, both in weight and lung capacity, of the nonsmokers, although they averaged 15 months older.

It has been said that the universal habit of smoking has made Germany "a spectacled nation." Tobacco greatly irritates the eyes, and injuriously affects the optic nerves. The eyes of boys who use cigarettes to excess grow dull and weak, and every feature shows the mark of the insidious poison. The face is pallid and haggard, the cheeks hollow, the skin drawn, there is a loss of frankness of expression, the eyes are shifty, the movements nervous and uncertain, and all this is but preliminary to the ultimate degradation and loss of self-respect which follow the victim of the cigarette habit, through years of misery and failure.

Side by side with physical deterioration there goes on a process of moral degeneration which robs the cigarette smoking boy of refinement, of manners. The moral depravity which follows cigarette habit is appalling. Lying, cheating, swearing, impurity, loss of courage and manhood, a complete dropping of life's standards, result from such indulgence.

Magistrate Crane, of New York City, says: "Ninety-nine out of a hundred boys between the ages of 10 and 17 years who come before me charged with crime have their fingers disfigured by yellow cigarette stains—I am not a crank on this subject, I do not care to pose as a reformer, but it is my opinion that cigarettes will do more than liquor to ruin boys. When you have arraigned before you boys hopelessly deaf through the excessive use of cigarettes, boys who have stolen their sisters' earnings, boys who absolutely refuse to work, who do nothing but gamble and steal, you cannot help seeing that there is some direct cause, and a great deal of this boyhood crime, is, in my mind, easy to trace to the deadly cigarette. There is something in the poison of the cigarette that seems to get into the system of the boy and to destroy all moral fiber."

He gives the following probable course of a boy who begins to smoke cigarettes: "First, cigarettes. Second, beer and liquors. Third, craps—petty gambling. Fourth, horse racing—gambling on a bigger scale. Fifth, larceny. Sixth, state prison."

Another New York City magistrate says: "Yesterday I had before me 35 boy prisoners. Thirty-three of them were confirmed cigarette smokers. Today, from a reliable source, I have made the grewsome discovery that two of the largest cigarette manufacturers soak their product in a weak solution of opium. The fact that out of 35 prisoners 33 smoked cigarettes might seem to indicate some direct connection between cigarettes and crime. And when it is announced on authority that most cigarettes are doped with opium, this connection is not hard to understand. Opium is like whisky—it creates an increasing appetite that grows with what it feeds upon. A growing boy who lets tobacco and opium get a hold upon his senses is never long in coming under the domination of whisky, too. Tobacco is the boy's easiest and most direct road to whisky. When opium is added, the young man's chance of resisting the combined forces and escaping physical, mental, and moral harm is slim, indeed."

I think the above statement regarding the use of opium by manufacturers is exaggerated. Yet we know that young men of great natural ability, everywhere, some of them in high positions, are constantly losing their grip, deteriorating, dropping back, losing their ambition, their push, their stamina, and their energy, because of the cigarette's deadly hold upon them.

Did you ever watch the gradual deterioration of the cigarette smoker, the gradual withdrawal of manliness and character, the fading out of purpose, the decline of ambition; the substitution of the beastly for the manly, the decline of the divine and the ascendency of the brute?

A very interesting study this, to watch the gradual withdrawal from the face of all that was manly and clean, and all that makes for success. We can see where purity left him and was gradually replaced by vulgarity, and where he began to be cursed by commonness.

We can see the point at which he could begin to do a bad job or a poor day's work without feeling troubled about it.

We can tell when he began to lose his great pride in his personal appearance, when he began to leave his room in the morning and to go to his work without being perfectly groomed. Only a little while before he would have been greatly mortified to have been seen by his employers and associates with slovenly dress; but now baggy trousers, unblackened shoes, soiled linen, frayed necktie do not trouble him.

He is not quite as conscientious about his work as he used to be. He can leave a half-finished job, and cut his hours and rob his employer a little here and there without being troubled seriously. He can write a slipshod letter. He isn't particular about his spelling, punctuation, or handwriting, as formerly. He doesn't mind a little deceit.

Vulgarity no longer shocks him. He does not blush at the unclean test. Womanhood is not as sacred to him as in his innocent days. He does not reverence women as formerly; and he finds himself laughing at the coarse jest and the common remarks about them among his associates, when once he would have resented and turned away in disgust.

Dr. Lewis Bremer, late physician at St. Vincent's Institute for the Insane says, "Basing my opinion upon my experience gained in private sanitariums and hospitals, I will broadly state that the boy who smokes cigarettes at seven will drink whisky at 14, take morphine at 25, and wind up at 30 with cocaine and the rest of the narcotics."

The saddest effects of cigarette smoking are mental. The physical signs of deterioration have their mental correspondences. Sir William Hamilton said: "There is nothing great in matter but man; there is nothing great in man but mind." The cigarette smoker takes man's distinguishing faculty and uncrowns it. He "puts an enemy in his mouth to steal away his brains."

Anything which impairs one's success capital, which cuts down his achievement and makes him a possible failure when he might have been a grand success, is a crime against him. Anything which benumbs the senses, deadens the sensibilities, dulls the mental faculties, and takes the edge off one's ability, is a deadly enemy, and there is nothing else which effects all this so quickly as the cigarette. It is said that within the past 50 years not a student at Harvard University who used tobacco has been graduated at the head of his class, although, on the average, five out of six use tobacco.

The symptoms of a cigarette victim resemble those of an opium eater. A gradual deadening, benumbing influence creeps all through the mental and moral faculties; the standards all drop to a lower level; the whole average of life is cut down, the victim loses that power of mental grasp, the grip of mind which he once had. In place of his former energy and vim and push, he is more and more inclined to take things easy and to slide along the line of the least resistance. He becomes less and less progressive. He dreams more and acts less. Hard work becomes more and more irksome and repulsive, until work seems drudgery to him.

Professor William McKeever, of the Kansas Agricultural College, in the course of his findings after an exhaustive study of "The Cigarette Smoking Boy" presents facts which are as appalling as they are undeniable:

"For the past eight years I have been tracing out the cigarette boy's biography and I have found that in practically all cases the lad began his smoking habit clandestinely and with little thought of its seriousness while the fond parents perhaps believed that their boy was too good to engage in such practice.

"I have tabulated reports of the condition of nearly 2,500 cigarette-smoking schoolboys, and in describing them physically my informants have repeatedly resorted to the use of such epithets as 'sallow,' 'sore-eyed,' 'puny,' 'squeaky-voiced,' 'sickly,' 'short-winded,' and 'extremely nervous.' In my tabulated reports it is shown that, out of a group of 25 cases of young college students, smokers, whose average age of beginning was 13, according to their own admissions they had suffered as follows: Sore throat, 4; weak eyes, 10; pain in chest, 8; 'short wind,' 21; stomach trouble, 10; pain in heart, 9. Ten of them appeared to be very sickly. The younger the boy, the worse the smoking hurts him in every way, for these lads almost invariably inhale the fumes; and that is the most injurious part of the practice."

Professor McKeever made hundreds of sphygmograph records of boys addicted to the smoking habit. Discussing what the records showed, he says:

"The injurious effects of smoking upon the boy's mental activities are very marked. Of the many hundreds of tabulated cases in my possession, several of the very youthful ones have been reduced almost to the condition of imbeciles. Out of 2,336 who were attending public school, only 6 were reported 'bright students.' A very few, perhaps 10, were 'average,' and all the remainder were 'poor' or 'worthless' as students. The average grades of 50 smokers and 50 nonsmokers were computed from the records of one term's work done in the Kansas Agricultural college and the results favored the latter group with a difference of 17.5 percent. The two groups represented the same class rank; that is, the same number of seniors, juniors, sophomores, and freshmen."

A thorough investigation of the effects of cigarette smoking on boys has been carried on in one of the San Francisco schools for many months. This investigation was ordered because a great many of the boys were inferior to the girls, both mentally and morally.

It was found that nearly three-fourths of the boys who smoked cigarettes had nervous disorders, while only one of those who did not smoke had any nervous symptoms. A great many of the cigarette smokers had defective hearing, while only one of those who did not smoke was so afflicted. A large percentage of the boys who smoked were defective in memory, while only one boy who did not smoke was so affected. A large portion of the boys who smoked were reported as low in deportment and morals, while only a very small percentage of those who did not smoke were similarly affected. It was found that the minds of many of the cigarette smokers could not comprehend or grasp ideas as quickly or firmly as those who did not smoke.

Nearly all of the cigarette smokers were found to be untidy and unclean in their personal appearance, and a great many of them were truants; but among those who did not smoke not a single boy had been corrected for truancy. Most of the smokers ranked very low in their studies as compared with those who did not smoke. Seventy-nine percent of them failed of promotion, while the percentage of failure among those who did not smoke was exceedingly small.

Of 20 boy smokers who were under careful observation for several months, 19 stood below the average of the class, while only two of those who did not smoke stood below. Very poor workers were 17 out of the 20 and they seemed absolutely incapable of close or continuous application to any of their studies.

Professor Wilkinson, principal of a leading high school, says, "I will not try to educate a boy with the cigarette habit. It is wasted time. The mental faculties of the boy who smokes cigarettes are blunted."

Another high school principal says, "Boys who smoke cigarettes are always backward in their studies; they are filthy in their personal habits, and coarse in their manners, they are hard to manage and dull in appearance."

It is apparent therefore that the cigarette habit disqualifies the student mentally, that it retards him in his studies, dwarfs his intellect, and leaves him far behind those of inferior mental equipment who do not indulge in the injurious use of tobacco in any form.

The mental, moral, and physical deterioration from the use of cigarettes, has been noted by corporations and employers of labor generally, until today the cigarette devotee finds himself barred from many positions that are open to those of inferior capabilities, who are not enslaved by the deadly habit.

Cigarette smoking is no longer simply a moral question. The great business world has taken it up as a deadly enemy of advancement, of achievement. Leading business firms all over the country have put the cigarette on the prohibited list. In Detroit alone, 69 merchants have agreed not to employ the cigarette user. In Chicago, Montgomery Ward and Company, Hibbard, Spencer and Bartlett, and some of the other large concerns have prohibited cigarette smoking among all employees under 18 years of age. Marshall Field and Company, and the Morgan and Wright Tire Company have this rule: "No cigarettes can be smoked by our employees." One of the questions on the application blanks at Wanamaker's reads: "Do you use tobacco or cigarettes?"

The superintendent of the Linden Street Railway, of St. Louis, says: "Under no circumstances will I hire a man who smokes cigarettes. He is as dangerous on the front of a motor as a man who drinks. In fact, he is more dangerous; his nerves are apt to give way at any moment. If I find a car running badly, I immediately begin to investigate to find if the man smokes cigarettes. Nine times out of ten he does, and then he goes, for good."

The late E. H. Harriman, head of the Union Pacific Railroad system, used to say that they "might as well go to a lunatic asylum for their employees as to hire cigarette smokers." The Union Pacific Railroad prohibits cigarette smoking among its employees.

The New York, New Haven, and Hartford, the Chicago, Rock Island, and Pacific, the Lehigh Valley, the Burlington, and many others of the leading railroad companies of this country have issued orders positively forbidding the use of cigarettes by employees while on duty.

Some time ago, 25 laborers working on a bridge were discharged by the roadmasters of the West Superior, Wisconsin Railroad because of cigarette smoking. The Pittsburg and Western Railroad, which is part of the Baltimore and Ohio system, gave orders forbidding the use of cigarettes by its employees on passenger trains and notified passengers that they must not smoke cigarettes in their coaches.

In the call issued for the competitive examination for messenger service in the Chicago post office, sometime since, 700 applicants were informed that only the best equipped boys were wanted for this service, and that under no circumstances would boys who smoked cigarettes be employed. Other post offices have taken a similar stand.

If someone should present you with a most delicately adjusted chronometer—one which would not vary a second in a year—do you think it would pay you to trifle with it, to open the case in the dust, to leave it out in the rain overnight, or to put in a drop of glue or a chemical which would ruin the delicacy of its adjustment so that it would no longer keep good time? Would you think it wise to take such chances?

But the Creator has given you a matchless machine, so delicately and wondrously made that it takes a quarter of a century to bring it to perfection, to complete growth, and yet you presume to trifle with it, to do all sorts of things which are infinitely worse than leaving your watch open out of doors overnight, or even in water.

The great object of the watch is to keep time. The supreme purpose of this marvelous piece of human machinery is power. The watch means nothing except time. If the human machinery does not produce power, it is of no use.

The merest trifle will prevent the watch from keeping time; but you think that you can put anything into your human machinery, that you can do all sorts of irrational things with it, and yet you expect it to produce power—to keep perfect time. It is important that the human machine shall be kept as responsive to the slightest impression or influence as possible, and the brain should be kept clear so that the thought may be sharp, biting, gripping, so that the whole mentality will act with efficiency. And yet you do not hesitate to saturate the delicate brain cells with vile drinks, to poison them with nicotine, to harden them with smoke from the vilest of weeds. You expect the man to turn out as exquisite work, to do the most delicate things to retain his exquisite sense of ability notwithstanding the hardening, the benumbing influence of cigarette poisoning.

Let the boy or youth who is tempted to indulge in the first cigarette ask himself—Can I afford to take this enormous risk? Can I jeopardize my health, my strength, my future, my all, by indulging in a practice which has ruined tens of thousands of promising lives?

Let the youth who is tempted say, "No! I will wait until mind and body are developed, until I have reached man's estate before I will begin to use tobacco." Experience proves that those who reach a robust manhood are rarely willing to sacrifice health and happiness to the cigarette habit.

Many years ago, an eminent physician and specialist in nervous diseases put himself on record as holding the firm belief that the evil effects of the use of tobacco were more lasting and far reaching than the injurious consequences that follow the excessive use of alcohol. Apart from affections of the throat and cancerous diseases of lips and tongue which frequently affect smokers there is a physical taint which is transmitted to offspring which handicaps the unfortunate infant "from its earliest breath."

The only salvation of the race, said this physician, lay in the fact that women did not smoke. If they too acquired the tobacco habit future generations would be stamped by the degeneracy and depravity which follow the use of tobacco as surely as they follow the use of alcohol.

In view of these facts the increase of cigarette smoking among women may well alarm those who have at heart the wellbeing of the rising generation. So rapidly has this habit spread that fashionable hotels and cafes are providing rooms for the especial use of those women who like to indulge in an after-dinner cigarette. A noted restaurant in New York recently added an annex to which ladies with their escorts might retire and smoke. We often see women smoking in New York hotels and restaurants.

Not long ago the writer was a guest at a dinner and to his surprise several ladies at the table lighted their cigarettes with as much composure as if it were the most natural thing in the world.

At a reception recently, I saw the granddaughter of one of America's greatest authors smoking cigarettes.

What a spectacle, to see a descendant so nearly removed from one of Nature's grandest noblemen, a princely gentleman, smoking! And I said to myself, "What would her grandfather think if he could see this?"

On a train running between London and Liverpool, a compartment especially reserved for women smokers has been provided. It is said that three American women were the cause of this innovation. The superintendent of one of our largest American railways says that he would not be surprised if the American roads were compelled to follow the lead of their English brethren.

It is not unreasonable to suppose that this addiction to the use of tobacco is in many cases inherited. A friend told me of a very charming young woman who was passionately devoted to tobacco. At a time when it was not usual for women to smoke in public her craving for a cigarette was so strong that she could not deny herself the indulgence. She said her father, a deacon in the church, had been an inveterate smoker, and her love of tobacco dated back to her earliest remembrance. Every woman should use the uttermost of her influence to discourage the use of the cigarette and enlist the girls as well as boys in her fight against the evil and injurious practice of cigarette smoking.

*Blessed are the pure in heart for they shall see God.
(Matthew 5:8)*

—Jesus

*My strength is as the strength of ten
Because my heart is pure.*

—Alfred, Lord Tennyson

Virtue alone raises us above hopes, fears, and chances.

—Seneca

*Even from the body's purity the mind
Receives a secret sympathetic aid.*

—James Thomson

THE POWER OF PURITY

Purity is a broad word with a deep meaning. It denotes far more than superficial cleanness. It goes below the surface of guarded speech and polite manners to the very heart of being. *"Out of the heart are the issues of life."* *(Proverbs 4:23)* Make the fountain clean and the waters that flow from it will be pure and limpid. Make the heart clean and the life will be clean.

Purity is defined as "free from contact with that which weakens, impairs or pollutes." How forceful then is the converse of the definition: Impurity weakens, impairs, and pollutes. It weakens both mind and body. It impairs the health. It pollutes not only the thoughts but the conduct which inevitably has its beginning and its end in thought.

Innocence is the state of natural purity. It was the state of Adam and Eve in the Garden of Eden. When they sinned *"they knew that they were naked."* *(Genesis 3:7b)* They lost innocence never to regain it. But purity may be attained. As an unclean garment may be washed, so the heart may be purified and made clean. Ghosts of past impurities still may dog us, but they are ghosts that may be laid with an imperative *"Get thee behind me, Satan."* *(Matthew 16:23b)* They are like the lions that affrighted Bunyan's pilgrim—chained securely. They may roar and threaten, but they are powerless if we deny their power. The man who is striving for purity wholeheartedly is like one who sits safely in a guarded house. Old memories of evil things like specters may peer in at the windows and mow and gibber at him, but they cannot touch him unless he gives them power, unless he unlocks the door of his heart and bids them enter.

As the lotus flower grows out of the mud, so may purity and beauty spring up from even the vilest past if we but will it so.

As purity is power so impurity is impotence, weakness, degeneracy.

Many a man goes on in an impure career thinking himself secure, thinking his secret hidden. But impurity, like murder, will out. There was a noted pugilist who was unexpectedly defeated in a great ring battle. People said the fight was a "fake," that it was a "put up job." But those who knew said "impurity." He had lived an evil, debauched life for several years, and he went into the ring impaired in strength, weakened by his transgressions of the law of pure living. Purity is power; impurity is weakness.

There is a saying of Scripture which is absolutely scientific: "Be sure your sin will find you out." (Numbers 32:23b) Note this; it is not that your sin will be found out, but your sin will find you out. Sin recoils on the sinner, and of all sins that surely find us out, the sins against purity are the most certain to bring retribution.

Young men do not think that listening to an off-color story, or anything that is vulgar, can injure them much, and, for fear of ridicule, they laugh when they hear anything of the kind, even when it is repulsive to them, and when they loathe it. It is a rare thing for a young man to express with emphasis his disapproval. To know life properly is to know the best in it, not the worst. No one ever yet was made stronger by his knowledge of impurity or experience in sin.

It is said that the mind's phonograph will faithfully reproduce a bad story even up to the point of death. Do not listen once. You can never get the stain entirely out of your life. Your character will absorb the poison. Impurity is especially fatal in its grip upon the young, because of the vividness of the youthful imagination and the facility with which insinuating suggestions enter the youthful thought.

Our court records show that a very large percentage of criminals began their downfall through the fatal contagion of impurity communicated from various associations.

Remember that you cannot tell what may come to you in the future, what honor or promotion; and you cannot afford to take chances upon having anything in your history which can come up to embarrass you or to keep you back. A thing which you now look upon as a bit of pleasure may come up in the future to hamper your progress. The thing you do today while trying to have a good time may come up to block your progress years afterwards.

I know men who have been thrust into positions of honor and public trust who would give anything in the world if they could blot out some of the unclean experiences of their youth. Things in their early history, which they had forgotten all about and which they never expected to hear from again, are raked up when they become candidates for office or positions of trust. These forgotten bits of so-called pleasure loom up in old life as insurmountable bars across their pathway.

I know a very rich young man who thought he was just having a good time in his youth—sowing his wild oats—who would give a large part of his vast wealth today if he could blot out a few years of his folly.

It seems strange that men will work hard to build a reputation, and then throw it all away by some weakness in their character. How many men there are in this country with great brain power, men who are kings in their specialties, men who have worked like slaves to achieve their aims, whose reputations have been practically ruined by the flaw of impurity!

Character is a record of our thoughts and acts. That which we think about most, the ideals and motives uppermost in our mind, are constantly solidifying into character. What we are constantly thinking about, and aiming toward and trying to obtain becomes a permanent part of the life.

The man whose thoughts are low and impure, very quickly gives this bent and tendency to his character.

The character levels itself with the thought, whether high or low. No man can have a pure, clean character who does not habitually have pure, clean thoughts. The immoral man is invariably an impure thinker—whatever we harbor in the mind outpictures itself in the body.

In Eastern countries the leper is compelled to cry, "Unclean, unclean," upon the approach of any one not so cursed. What a blessing to humanity if our modern moral lepers were compelled to cry, "Unclean, unclean," before they approach innocent victims with their deadly contagion!

About the vilest thing on earth is a human being whose character is so tainted with impurity that he leaves the slimy trail of the serpent wherever he goes.

There never was a more beautiful and pathetic prayer than that of the poor soiled, brokenhearted psalmist in his hour of shame, *"Create in me a clean heart." (Psalms 51:10a) "Who shall ascend into the hill of the Lord, who shall stand in His holy place? He that hath clean hands and a pure heart." (Psalms 24:3–4a)* There are thousands of men who would cut off their right hands today to be free from the stain, the poison, of impurity.

There can be no lasting greatness without purity. Vice honeycombs the physical strength as well as destroys the moral fiber. Now and again some man of note topples with a crash to sudden ruin. Yet the cause of the moral collapse is not sudden. There has been a slow undermining of virtue going on probably for years; then, in an hour when honor, truth, or honesty is brought to a crucial test, the weakened character gives way and there is an appalling commercial or social crash which often finds an echo in the revolver shot of the suicide.

Tennyson shows the effect of Launcelot's guilty love for Guinevere, in the great knight's conscious loss of power. His wrongful passion indirectly brought about the death of fair Elaine. He himself at times shrank from puny men wont to go down before the shadow of his spear. Like a scarlet blot his sin stains all his greatness, and he muses on it remorsefully:

> *For what am I? What profits me my name*
> *Of greatest knight? I fought for it and have it.*
> *Pleasure to have it, none; to lose it pain;*
> *Now grown a part of me: but what use in it?*
> *To make men worse by making my sin known?*
> *Or sin seem less, the sinner seeming great?*

Later when the knights of the Round Table joined in the search for the Holy Grail, that lost sacred vessel,

> *The cup, the cup itself from which our Lord*
> *Drank at the last sad supper with his own,*

Launcelot was overtaken by his sin and failed ignominiously. Only Galahad the Pure was permitted to see the cup unsurrounded by a blinding glory, a fearful splendor of watching eyes and guarding shapes.

No one is quite the same in his own estimation when he has been once guilty of contact with impurity. His self-respect has suffered a loss.

Something has gone out of his life. His own good opinion of himself has suffered deterioration, and he can never face his life task with quite the same confidence again. Somehow, he feels that the world will know of his soul's debauch and judge him accordingly.

There is nothing which will mar a life more quickly than the consciousness of a soul stain. The loss of self-respect, the loss of character, is irreparable.

We are beginning to find that there is an intimate connection between absolute purity of one's thought and life and his good health, good thinking, and good work, a very close connection between the moral faculties and the physical health; that nothing so exhausts vitality and vitiates the quality of work and ideals, so takes the edge off of one's ambition, dulls the brain and aspiration, as impurity of thought and life. It seems to blight all the faculties and to demoralize the whole man, so that his efficiency is very much lessened. He does not speak with the same authority. The air of the conqueror disappears from his manner. He does not think so clearly; he does not act with so great certainty, and his self-faith is lost, because confidence is based upon self-respect, and he can no longer respect himself when he does things which he would not respect in another.

The fact that his impure acts are done secretly makes no difference. No one can thoroughly respect himself when he does that which demoralizes him, which is unbecoming a gentleman, no matter whether other people know it or not. Impurity blights everything it touches.

It is not enough to be thought pure and clean and sound. One must actually be pure and clean and sound morally, or his self-respect is undermined.

Purity is power because it means integrity of thought, integrity of conduct. It means wholeness. The impure man cannot be a great power, because he cannot thoroughly believe in himself when conscious that he is rotten in any part of his nature. Impurity works like leaven, which affects everything in a man. The very consciousness that the impurity is working within him robs him of power.

Apart from the moral side of this question, let us show how these things affect one's success in life by sapping the energies, weakening the nature, lowering one's standards, blurring one's ideals, discouraging one's ambition, and lessening one's vitality and power.

In the last analysis of success, the mainspring of achievement must rest in the strength of one's vitality, for, without a stock of health equal to great emergencies and persistent longevity, even the greatest ambition is comparatively powerless. And there is nothing that will sap the life forces so quickly as dissipation and impure living.

Is there anything truer than that "To be carnally minded is death?" If the thought is carnal, the body must correspond, must express it in some physical discord.

Nothing else will destroy the very foundations of vitality quicker than impurity of thought and animal self-indulgence. The ideals must be kept bright and the ambition clean-cut.

Purity of thought means that the mental processes are not clouded, muddy, or clogged by brain ash from a dissipated life, from violation of the laws of health. Pure thought comes from pure blood, and pure blood from a clean, sane life. Purity signifies a great deal besides freedom from sensual taint. It means saneness, purity, and quality.

It has been characteristic of great leaders, men whose greatness has stood the acid test of time, that they have been virtuous in conduct, pure in thought.

"I have such a rich story that I want to tell you," said an officer, who one evening came into the Union camp in a rollicking mood. "There are no ladies present, are there?"

General Grant, lifting his eyes from the paper which he was reading, and looking the officer squarely in the eye, said slowly and deliberately:

"No, but there are gentlemen present."

"A great trait of Grant's character," said George W. Childs, "was his purity. I never heard him express an impure thought, or make an indelicate allusion in any way or shape. There is nothing I ever heard him say that could not be repeated in the presence of women. If a man was brought up for an appointment, and it was shown that he was an immoral man, Grant would not appoint him, no matter how great the pressure brought to bear."

On one occasion, when Grant formed one of a dinner party of Americans in a foreign city, conversation drifted into references to questionable affairs, when he suddenly rose and said, "Gentlemen, please excuse me, I will retire."

It is the glory of a man to have clean lips and a clean mind. It is the glory of a woman not to know evil, even in her thoughts.

Isaac Newton's most intimate friend in young manhood was a noted foreign chemist. They were constant associates until one day the Italian told an impure story, after which Newton never would associate with him.

"My extreme youth, when I took command of the army of Italy," said Napoleon, "rendered it necessary that I should evince great reserve of manners and the utmost severity of morals. This was indispensable to enable me to sustain authority over men so greatly my superiors in age and experience. I pursued a line of conduct in the highest degree irreproachable and exemplary. In spotless morality I was a Cato, and must have appeared such to all. I was a philosopher and a sage. My supremacy could be retained only by proving myself a better man than any other man in the army. Had I yielded to human weakness, I should have lost my power."

The military antagonist and conqueror of Napoleon, the Duke of Wellington, was a man of simple life and austere virtue. When he was laid to rest in the crypt of St. Paul's Cathedral, "in streaming London's central roar," the poet who wrote his funeral ode was able to say of him:

Whatever record leap to light
He never shall be shamed.

The peril of impurity lies in the insidiousness of the poison. Just one taint of impurity, one glance at a lewd picture, one hearing of an unclean story may begin the fatal corruption of mind and heart.

It is the little rift within the lute
That by and by will make the music mute,
The little rift within the lover's lute
Or little pitted speck in garnered fruit
That rotting inward slowly molders all.

When Bunyan's pilgrim was assailed by temptation, he stopped his ears with his fingers and fled for his life. Let the young man who values himself, who sets store upon health and has ambition to succeed in his chosen career, be deaf to unclean speech and flee the companionship of those who think and speak uncleanness.

It is the experience of every man who has forsaken vice and turned his feet into the paths of virtue that evil memories will, in his holiest hours, leap upon him like a lion from ambush. Into the harmony of the hymn, he sings memory will interpolate unbidden, the words of some sensual song. Pictures of his debauches, his past licentiousness, will fill his vision, and the unhappy victim can only beat upon his breast and cry, "Me miserable! Whither shall I flee?" This has been, through all time, the experience of the men that have sought sanctity in seclusion. The saints, the hermits in their caves, the monks in their cells, could never escape the obsessions of memory which with horrible realism and scorching vividness revived past scenes of sin.

A boy once showed to another a book of impure words and pictures. He to whom the book was shown had it in his hands only a few minutes. In old age he held high office in the church, and years and years afterwards told a friend that he would give half he possessed had he never seen it, because its impure images, at the most holy times, would arise unbidden to his mind.

Physicians tell us that every particle of the body changes in a very few years; but no chemistry, human or divine, can entirely expunge from the mind a bad picture. Like the paintings buried for centuries in Pompeii, without the loss of tint or shade, these pictures are as brilliant in age as in youth.

Association begets assimilation. We cannot mix with evil associations without being contaminated; cannot touch pitch without being defiled. Impurity is especially fatal in its grip upon the young, because of the vividness of the youthful imagination and the facility with which insinuating suggestions enter the youthful thought.

Indelible and satanic is the taint of the evil suggestive power which a lewd, questionable picture or story leaves upon the mind. Nothing else more fatally mars the ideals of life and lowers the standard of manhood and womanhood.

To read writers whose lines express the utmost possible impurity so dexterously and cunningly that not a vulgar word is used, but rosy, glowing, suggestive language—authors who soften evil and show deformity with the tints of beauty. What is this but to take the feet out of the straight road into the guiltiest path of seduction?

Very few realize the power of a diseased imagination to ruin a precious life. Perhaps the defect began in a little speck of taint. No other faculty has such power to curse or bless mankind, to build up or tear down, to ennoble or debauch, to make happy or miserable, or has such power upon our destiny, as the imagination.

Many a ruined life began its downfall in the dry rot of a perverted imagination. How little we realize that by subtle, moral manufacture, repeated acts of the imagination weave themselves into a mighty tapestry, every figure and fancy of which will stand out in living colors in the character web of our lives, to approve or condemn us.

In many cases where, for no apparent reason, one is making failure after failure, never reaching, even approximately, the position which was anticipated for him, if he would look frankly into his own heart, and searchingly at his own secret habits, he would find that which, hidden, like the worm at the heart of the rose, is destroying and making impossible all that ennobles, beautifies, and enriches life.

"I solemnly warn you," says Beecher, "against indulging a morbid imagination. In that busy and mischievous faculty begins the evil. Were it not for his airy imagination, man might stand his own master—not overmatched by the worst part of himself. But ah! these summer reveries, these venturesome dreams, these fairy castles, builded for no good purposes—they are haunted by impure spirits, who will fascinate, bewitch, and corrupt you. Blessed are the pure in heart. Blessed art thou, most favored of God, whose THOUGHTS are chastened; whose imagination will not breathe or fly in tainted air, and whose path hath been measured by the golden reed of purity."

To be pure in heart is the youth's first great commandment. Do not listen to men who tell you that "vice is a necessity." Nothing is a necessity that is wrong—that debauches self-respect. "All wickedness is weakness." Vice and vigor have nothing in common. Purity is strength, health, power.

Do not imagine that impurity can be hidden! One may as well expect to have consumption or any other deadly disease, and to look and appear healthy, as to be impure in thought and mind, and to look and appear manly and noble souled. Character writes its record in the flesh.

"No, no, these are not trifles," said George Whitefield, when a friend asked why he was so particular to bathe frequently, and always have his linen scrupulously clean; "a minister must be without spot, even in his garments." Purity in a good man cannot be carried too far.

There is a permanency in the stamp left by the sins resulting from impure thought that follows even to the grave. Diseases unnameable, the consequences of the Scarlet Sin, the following after the "strange woman," write their record in the very bones, literally fulfilling the Scripture statement: *"Their sins shall lie down with their bones in the dust." (Job 20:11)*

We often detect in the eye and in the manner the black leper spots of impurity long before the youth suspect they have ever been noticed. When there is a scar or a stain upon one's self-respect it is bound to appear on the surface sooner or later. What fearful blots and stains are left on the characters of those who have to fight for a lifetime to rid themselves of a blighting and contaminating influence, moral or physical!

Chemists tell us that scarlet is the only color which cannot be bleached. There is no known chemical which can remove it. So, formerly, scarlet rags were made into blotting paper. When the sacred writer wished to emphasize the power of Divine forgiveness, of Divine love, he said: *"Even though thy sins be as scarlet, they shall be made white as wool!" (Isaiah 1:18)* It certainly takes omnipotent power to expunge impurity from the mind. There is certainly one sin which only Divine power can bleach out of the character—the sin of impurity.

No man can think much of himself when he is conscious of impurity anywhere in his life. And the very knowledge that one is absolutely pure in his thought and clean in his life increases his self-respect and his self-faith wonderfully.

It is a terrible handicap to be conscious that, however much others may think of us, we are foul inside, that our thoughts are vile. It does not matter that our vicious acts are secret, we cannot cover them.

Whatever we have thought or done will outpicture itself in the expression, in the bearing. It will be hung out upon the bulletin board of the face and manner for the world to read. We instinctively feel a person's reality; not what he pretends, but what he is, for we radiate our reality, which often contradicts our words.

There is only one panacea for impurity. Constant occupation and pure, high thinking are absolutely necessary to a clean life.

"I should be a poor counselor of young men," wrote a true friend of youth, "if I taught you that purity is possible only by isolation from the world. We do not want that sort of holiness which can thrive only in seclusion; we want that virile, manly purity which keeps itself unspotted from the world, even amid its worst debasements, just as the lily lifts its slender chalice of white and gold to heaven, untainted by the soil in which it grows, though that soil be the reservoir of death and putrefaction."

Impurity is the forfeiture of manliness. The true man must be untarnished. James went so far as to declare that this is just what religion is: *"Pure religion and undefiled before God and the Father is this...to keep himself unspotted from the world." (James 1:27)*

Every true man shrinks from uncleanness. He knows what it means. Impurity makes lofty friendships impossible. It robs all of life's intercourse of its freshness and its joyous innocence. It sullies all beauty. It does these things chiefly because it separates men from God and His vision. The best and holiest is barred to the stained man. Impurity makes it impossible for him to appreciate what is pure and fine, dulls his finer perceptions, and he is not given the place where only pure and fine things are.

Helen Keller

There can be no such thing as an impure gentleman. The two words contradict each other. A gentleman must be pure. He need not have fine clothes. He may have had few advantages. But he must be pure and clean. And, if he has all outward grace and gift and be inwardly unclean, though he may call himself a gentleman, he is a liar and a lie.

O, young man, guard your heart purity! Keep innocence! Never lose it; if it be gone, you have lost from the casket the most precious gift of God. The first purity of imagination, of thought, and of feeling, if soiled, can be cleansed by no fuller's soap. If a harp be broken, art may repair it; if a light be quenched, the flame may kindle it; but if a flower be crushed, what art can repair it? If an odor be wafted away, who can collect or bring it back?

Parents are, in many cases, responsible for the impurity of their children. Through a mistaken sense of delicacy, they allow the awakened, searching mind of the child to get information concerning its physical nature from the mind of some boy or girl no better taught than itself, and so conceive wholly wrong and harmful ideas concerning things of which it is vitally important that every human being should at the outset of life have clear and adequate ideas. Such silence, many times, is fatal, and always foolish, if not criminal.

"I have noticed," says William Acton, "that all patients who have confessed to me that they have practiced vice, lamented that they were not, when children, made aware of its consequences; and I have been pressed over and over again to urge on parents, guardians, schoolmasters, and others interested in the education of youth, the necessity of giving to their charges some warning, some intimation, of their danger. To parents and guardians, I offer my earnest advice that they should, by hearty sympathy and frank explanation, aid their charges in maintaining pure lives." What stronger breastplate than a heart untainted?

A prominent writer says: "If young persons poison their bodies and corrupt their minds with vicious courses, no lapse of time, after a reform, is likely to restore them to physical soundness and the soul purity of their earlier days."

There is one idea concerning purity which should never have been conceived, and, having been conceived, should be, once and forever, eternally exploded. It is that purity is different in the different sexes.

It would be loosening the foundations of virtue to countenance the notion that, because of a difference in sex, men are at liberty to set morality at defiance, and to do with impunity that which, if done by a woman, would stain her character for life. To maintain a pure and virtuous condition of society, therefore, man as well as woman must be virtuous and pure, both alike shunning all acts infringing on the heart, character, and conscience—shunning them as poison, which, once imbibed, can never be entirely thrown out again.

Is there any reason why a man should have any license to drag his thoughts through the mud and filth any more than a woman? Is there any sex in principle? Isn't a stain a blot upon a boy's character just as bad as upon a girl's? If purity is so refining and elevating for one sex, why should it not be for the other?

It is incredible that a man should be socially ostracized for comparatively minor offenses, yet be rotten with immorality and be received into the best homes. But, if a woman makes the least false step in this direction, she is not only ostracized but treated with the utmost contempt, while the man who was the chief sinner in causing a woman's downfall, society will pardon.

To put it on the very lowest ground, I am certain that if young men knew and realized the fearful risks to health that they take by indulging in gross impurities they would put them by with a shudder of disgust and aversion. It may very easily happen—it very often actually does happen—that one single step from the path of purity clouds a man's whole life with misery and unspeakable suffering; and not only that, but even entails lifelong disease on children yet unborn.

To return to its Maker at the close of life the marvelous body which He gave us, scarred by a heedless life, with the heart rotten with impurity, the imagination filled with vicious images, the character honeycombed with vice, is a most ungrateful return for the priceless life of opportunity.

A mind retaining all the dew and freshness of innocence shrinks from the very idea of impurity, the very suggestion of it, as if it were sin to have even thought or heard of it, as if even the shadow of the evil would leave some soil on the unsullied whiteness of the virgin mind. "When modesty is once extinguished, it knows not a return."

THE HABIT OF HAPPINESS

The highest happiness must always come from the exercise of the best thing in us.

When you find happiness in anything but useful work, you will be the first man or woman to make the discovery.

If you take an inventory of yourself at the very outset of your career you will find that you think you are going to find happiness in things or in conditions. Most people think they are going to find the largest part of their happiness in money, what money will buy or what it will give them in the way of power, influence, comforts, luxuries. They think they are going to find a great deal of their happiness in marriage. How quickly they find that the best happiness they will ever know is that which must be limited to their own capacity for enjoyment, that their happiness cannot come from anything outside of them but must be developed from within.

Many people believe they are going to find much of their happiness in books, in travel, in leisure, in freedom from the thousand and one anxieties and cares and worries of business; but the moment they get in the position where they thought they would have freedom many other things come up in their minds and cut off much of the expected joy. When they get money and leisure, they often find that they are growing selfish, which cuts off a lot of their happiness.

No man able to work can be idle without feeling a sense of guilt at not doing his part in the world, for every time he sees the poor laboring people who are working for him, who are working everywhere, he is constantly reminded of his meanness in shifting upon others what he is able to do and ought to do himself. Idleness is the last place to look for happiness. Idleness is like a stagnant pool. The moment the water ceases to flow, to work, to do something, all sorts of vermin and hideous creatures develop in it. It becomes torpid and unhealthy giving out miasma and repulsive odors. In the same way work is the only thing that will keep the individual healthy and wholesome and clean. An idle brain very quickly breeds impurities.

The married man quickly learns that his domestic happiness depends upon what he himself contributes to the partnership, that he cannot take out a great deal without putting a great deal in, for selfishness always reaps a mean, despicable harvest. It is only the generous giver who gets much. There is nothing which will so shrivel up a man; and contract his capacity for happiness as selfishness. It is always a fatal blighter, blaster, disappointer. We must give to get, we must be great before we can get great enjoyment; great in our motive, grand in our endeavor, sublime in our ideas.

It is impossible, absolutely unscientific, for a bad person to be truly happy; just as impossible as it would be for one to be comfortable while lying on a bed of nettles which are constantly pricking him. There is no way under heaven by which a person can be really happy without being good, clean, square, and true. This does not mean that a person is happy because he does not use tobacco, drink, gamble, use profane language or does not do other vicious things. Some of the meanest, narrowest, most contemptible people in the world do none of these things but they are uncharitable, jealous, envious, revengeful. They stab you in the back, slander you, cheat you. They may be cunning, underhanded, and yet have a good standing in the church.

No person can be really happy who has a small, narrow, bigoted, uncharitable mind or disposition. Generosity, charity, kindness are absolutely essential to real happiness. Deceitful people cannot be happy; they cannot respect themselves because they inwardly despise themselves for deceiving you. A person must be open minded, transparent, simple, in order to be really happy. A person who is always covering up something, trying to keep things from you, misleading you, deceiving you, cannot get away from self-reproach, and hence cannot be really happy.

Selfishness is a fatal enemy of happiness because no one ever does a really selfish thing without feeling really mean, without despising himself for it. I have never seen a strong young man sneak into a vacant seat in a car and allow an old man or woman with a package or a baby in her arms to stand, without looking as though he knew he had done a mean, selfish thing. There is a look of humiliation in his face. We are so constituted that we cannot help condemning ourselves for our mean or selfish acts.

The liar is never really happy. He is always on nettles lest his deceit betray him. He never feels safe. Dishonesty in all its phases is fatal to happiness, for no dishonest person can get his self-approval. Without this no happiness is possible.

Before you can be really happy, my friend, you must be able to look back upon a well-spent past, a conscientious, unselfish past. If not, you will be haunted by demons which will destroy your happiness. If you have been mean and selfish, greedy and dishonest with your fellowmen, all sorts of horrible things will rise out of your money pile to terrify and to make your happiness impossible.

In other words, happiness is merely a result of the life work. It will partake of the exact quality of the motive which you have put into your life work. If these motives have been selfish, greedy, grasping, if cunning and dishonesty have dominated in your career, your happiness will be marred accordingly.

You cannot complain of your happiness, because it is your own child, the product of your own brain, your own effort. It has been made up of your motives, colored by your life aim. It exactly corresponds to the cause which produced it.

There is the greatest difference in the world between the happiness which comes from a sweet, beautiful, unselfish, helpful, sympathetic, industrious, honorable career, and the mean satisfaction which may grow to be a part of your marked self if you have lived a selfish, grasping life.

What we call happiness is the harvest from our life sowing, our habitual thought sowing, deed doing. If we have sown selfish, envious, jealous, revengeful, hateful seeds, greedy, grasping seeds, we cannot expect a golden happiness harvest like that which comes from a clean and unselfish, helpful sowing.

If our harvest is full of the rank, poisonous weeds of jealousy, envy, dishonesty, cunning, and cruelty, we have no one to blame but ourselves, for we sowed the seed which produced that sort of a harvest.

Somehow some people have an entirely wrong idea of what real happiness is. They seem to think it can be bought, can be had by influence, that it can be purchased by money; that if they have money, they can get that wonderful, mysterious thing which they call happiness.

But happiness is a natural, faithful harvest from our sowing. It would be as impossible for selfish seed, greed seed to produce a harvest of contentment, of genuine satisfaction, of real joy, as for thistle seeds to produce a harvest of wheat or corn.

Whatever the quality of your enjoyment or happiness may be, you have patterned it by your life motive by the spirit in which you have worked, by the principles which have actuated you.

A pretty different harvest, I grant, many of us must face, marred with all sorts of hideous, poisonous weeds, but they are all the legitimate product of our sowing. No one can rob us of our harvest or change it very much. Every thought, every act, every motive, whether secret or public, is a seed which no power on earth can prevent going to its harvest of beauty or ugliness, honor or shame. Most people have an idea that happiness is something that can be manufactured. They do not realize that it can no more be manufactured than wheat or corn can be manufactured. It must be grown, and the harvest will be like the seed.

You, young man, make up your mind at the very outset of your career that whatever comes to you in life, that whether you succeed or fail, whether you have this or that, there is one thing you will have, and that is a happy, contented mind, that you will extract your happiness as you go along. You will not take the chances of picking up or developing the happy habit after you get rich, for then you may be too old.

Most people postpone their enjoyment until they are disappointed to find the power of enjoyment has largely gone by and that even if they had the means they could not get anything like as much real happiness out of it as they could have gotten as they went along when they were younger. Take no chances with your happiness, or the sort of a life that can produce it; whatever else you risk, do not risk this. Early form the happy habit, the habit of enjoyment every day, no matter what comes or does not come to you during the day. Pick crumbs of comfort out of your situation, no matter how unpleasant or disagreeable.

I know a man who, although poor, can manage to get more comfort out of a real tough, discouraging situation than anyone else I have ever seen. I have often seen him when he did not have a dollar to his name, with a wife to support; yet he was always buoyant, happy, cheerful, consented. He would even make fun out of an embarrassing situation, see something ludicrous in his extreme poverty.

There have never been such conflicting estimates, such varying ideas, regarding any state of human condition as to what constitutes happiness. Many people think that it is purchasable with money, but many of the most restless, discontented, unhappy people in the world are rich. They have the means of purchasing what they thought would produce happiness, but the real thing eludes them. On the other hand, some of the poorest people in the world are happy. The fact is that there is no possible way of cornering or purchasing happiness for it is absolutely beyond the reach of money. It is true, we can purchase a few comforts and immunities from some annoyances and worries with money which we cannot get without it. On the other hand, the great majority of people who have inherited money are positively injured by it, because it often stops their own development by taking away the motive for self-effort and self-reliance.

When people get money, they often stop growing because they depend upon the money instead of relying upon their own inherent resources.

Rich people suffer from their indulgences more than poor ones suffer from their hardships.

A great many rich people die with liver and kidney troubles which are effected both by eating and drinking. The kidneys are very susceptible to the presence of alcohol. If rich people try to get greater enjoyment out of life than poor people by eating and drinking, they are likely very quickly to come to grief. If they try to seek it through the avenue of leisure, they soon find that an idle brain is one of the most dangerous things in the world—nothing deteriorates faster. The mind was made for continual strong action, systematic, vigorous exercise, and this is possible only when some dominating aim and a great life purpose leads the way.

No person can be really healthful whose mind is not usefully and continually employed. So, there is no possibility of finding real happiness in idleness if we are able to work. Nature brings a wonderful compensatory power to those who are crippled or sick or otherwise disabled from working, but there is no compensation for idleness in those who are able to work. Nature only gives us the use of faculties we employ. "Use or lose" is her motto, and when we cease to use a faculty or function it is gradually taken away from us, gradually shrivels and atrophies.

There is no satisfaction like that which comes from the steady, persistent, honest, conscientious pursuit of a noble aim. There are a multitude of evidences in man's very structure that his marvelous mechanism was intended for action, for constant exercise, and that idleness and stagnation always mean deterioration and death of power. No man can remain idle without shrinking, shriveling, constantly becoming a less efficient man; for he can keep up only those faculties and powers which he constantly employs, and there is no other possible way. Nature puts her ban of deterioration and loss of power upon idleness. We see these victims everywhere shorn of power— weak, nerveless, backboneless, staminaless, gritless people, without forcefulness, mere nonentities because they have ceased working. Without work mental health is impossible and without health the fullest happiness is impossible.

It has been said that happiness is the most delusive thing that man pursues. Yet why need it be a blind search?

If we were to stop the first hundred people we meet on the street and ask them what in their experience has given them the most happiness, probably the answer of no two would be alike.

How interesting and instructive it would be to give a thousand dollars to each of these hundred people, and without their knowing it, follow them and see what they would do with the money—what it would mean to them.

To some poor youth hungry for an education, with no opportunity to gain it, this money would mean a college education. Another would see in his money a more comfortable home for his aged parents. To another this money would suggest all sorts of dissipation. Some would see books and leisure for self-improvement, a trip abroad.

We all wear different colored glasses and no two see life with the same tint.

Some find their present happiness in coarse dissipation; others in a quiet nook with a book. Some find their greatest happiness in friends, in social intercourse; others seek happiness in roving over the earth, always thinking that the greatest enjoyment is in another day, in another place, a little further on, in the next room, or tomorrow, or in another country.

To many people, happiness is never where they are, but almost anywhere else.

Most people lose sight of the simplicity of happiness. They look for it in big, complicated things. Real happiness is perfectly simple. In fact, it is incompatible with complexity. Simplicity is its very essence.

I was dining recently with a particularly successful young man who is trying very hard to be happy, but he takes such a complicated, strenuous view of everything that his happiness is always flying from him. He drives everything so fiercely, his life is so vigorous, so complicated, that happiness cannot find a home with him very long. Nor does he understand why. He has money, health; but he always has that restless faraway, absentminded gaze into something beyond, and I do not think he is ever really very happy. His whole manner of living is extremely complex. He does not seem to know where to find happiness. He has evidently mistaken the very nature of happiness. He thinks it consists in making a great show, in having great possessions, in doing things which attract a great deal of attention; but happiness would be strangled, suffocated in such an environment. The essentials of real happiness are few, simple, and close at hand.

Happiness is made up of very simple ingredients. It flees from the complex life. It evades pomp and show. The heart would starve amid the greatest luxuries.

Simple joys and the treasures of the heart and mind make happiness.

Happiness has very little to do with material things. It is a mental state of mind. Real permanent happiness cannot be found in mere temporary things, because its roots reach away down into eternal principles.

One of the most pathetic pictures in civilization is the great army of men and women searching the world over for happiness, as though it existed in things rather than in a state of mind.

The people who have spent years and a fortune trying to find it look as hungry and as lean of contentment and all that makes life desirable as when they started out. Chasing happiness all over the world is about as silly a business as any human being ever engaged in, for it was never yet found by any pursuer. Yet happiness is the simplest thing in the world. It is found in many a home with carpetless floors and pictureless walls. It knows neither rank, station, nor color, nor does it recognize wealth. It only demands that it live with a contented mind and pure heart. It will not live with ostentation; it flees from pretense; it loves the simple life; it insists upon a sweet, healthful, natural environment. It hates the forced and complicated and formal.

Real happiness flees from the things that pass away; it abides only in principle, permanency.

I have never seen a person who has lived a grasping, greedy, money-chasing life, who was not disappointed at what money has given him for his trouble.

It is only in giving, in helping, that we find our quest. Everywhere we go we see people who are disappointed, chagrined, shocked, to find that what they thought would be the angel of happiness turned out to be only a ghost.

All the misery and the crime of the world rest upon the failure of human beings to understand the principle that no man can really be happy until he harmonizes with the best thing in him, with the divine, and not with the brute. No one can be happy who tries to harmonize his life with his animal instincts. The God (the good) in him is the only possible thing that can make him happy.

Real happiness cannot be bribed by anything sordid or low. Nothing mean or unworthy appeals to it. There is no affinity between them. Founded upon principle, it is as scientific as the laws of mathematics, and he who works his problem correctly will get the happiness answer.

There is only one way to secure the correct answer to a mathematical problem; and that is to work in harmony with mathematical laws. It would not matter if half the world believed there was some other way to get the answer, it would never come until the law was followed with the utmost exactitude.

It does not matter that the great majority of the human race believe there is some other way of reaching the happiness goal. The fact that they are discontented, restless, and unhappy shows that they are not working their problem scientifically.

We are all conscious that there is another man inside of us, that there accompanies us through life a divine, silent messenger, that other, higher, better self, which speaks from the depths of our nature and which gives its consent, its "amen" to every right action, and condemns every wrong one.

Man is built upon the plan of honesty, of rectitude—the divine plan. When he perverts his nature by trying to express dishonesty, chicanery, and cunning, of course he cannot be happy.

The very essence of happiness is honesty, sincerity, truthfulness. He who would have real happiness for his companion must be clean, straightforward, and sincere. The moment he departs from the right she will take wings and fly away.

It is just as impossible for a person to reach the normal state of harmony while he is practicing selfish, grasping methods, as it is to produce harmony in an orchestra with instruments that are all jangled and out of tune. To be happy, we must be in tune with the infinite within us, in harmony with our better selves. There is no way to get around it.

There is no tonic like that which comes from doing things worthwhile. There is no happiness like that which comes from doing our level best every day, everywhere; no satisfaction like that which comes from stamping superiority, putting our royal trademark upon everything which goes through our hands.

Recently a rich young man was asked why he did not work. "I do not have to," he said. "Do not have to" has ruined more young men than almost anything else. The fact is, Nature never made any provision for the idle man. Vigorous activity is the law of life; it is the saving grace, the only thing that can keep a human being from retrograding. Activity along the line of one's highest ambition is the normal state of man, and he who tries to evade it pays the penalty in deterioration of faculty, in paralysis of efficiency. Do not flatter yourself that you can be really happy unless you are useful. Happiness and usefulness were born twins. To separate them is fatal.

It is as impossible for a human being to be happy who is habitually idle as it is for a fine chronometer to be normal when not running. The highest happiness is the feeling of wellbeing which comes to one who is actively employed doing what he was made to do, carrying out the great life purpose patterned in his individual bent. The practical fulfilling of the life purpose is to man what the actual running and keeping time are to the watch. Without action both are meaningless.

Man was made to do things. Nothing else can take the place of achievement in his life. Real happiness without achievement of some worthy aim is unthinkable. One of the greatest satisfactions in this world is the feeling of enlargement, of growth, of stretching upward and onward. No pleasure can surpass that which comes from the consciousness of feeling one's horizon of ignorance being pushed farther and farther away—of making headway in the world—of not only getting on, but also of getting up.

Happiness is incompatible with stagnation. A man must feel his expanding power lifting, tugging away at a lofty purpose, or he will miss the joy of living.

The discords, the bickerings, the divorces, the breaking up of rich homes, and the resorting to all sorts of silly devices by many rich people in their pursuit of happiness, prove that it does not dwell with them, that happiness does not abide with low ideals, with selfishness, idleness, and discord. It is a friend of harmony, of truth, of beauty, of affection, of simplicity.

Multitudes of men have made fortunes, but have murdered their capacity for enjoyment in the process. How often we hear the remark, "He has the money, but cannot enjoy it."

A man can have no greater delusion than that he can spend the best years of his life coining all of his energies into dollars, neglecting his home, sacrificing friendships, self-improvement, and everything else that is really worthwhile, for money, and yet find happiness at the end!

The happiness habit is just as necessary to our best welfare as the work habit, or the honesty or square-dealing habit. No one can do his best, his highest thing, who is not perfectly normal, and happiness is a fundamental necessity of our being. It is an indication of health, of sanity, of harmony. The opposite is a symptom of disease, of abnormality.

There are plenty of evidences in the human economy that we were intended for happiness, that it is our normal condition; that suffering, unhappiness, discontent, are absolutely foreign and abnormal to our natures. There is no doubt that our life was intended to be one grand, sweet song. We are built upon the plan of harmony, and every form of discord is abnormal.

There is something wrong when any human being in this world, tuned to infinite harmonies and beauties that are unspeakable, is unhappy and discontented.